tales

STORYTELLER'S SUPPER

written by
TAFFY THOMAS MBE

illustrated by
DOTTY KULTYS

DEDICATION

To all the storytellers, chefs and home cooks who have fed me along the way and shown me the joy and comfort to be found in the sharing of food and stories at our tables.

Writing this collection during the pandemic of 2020, it became clear that we were all rediscovering the importance of the simple gifts we share and often overlook. Provisions, care, the joy to be found in nature, all became an invaluable part of our lockdown survival. Many people kept on working to ensure that these needs were provided, so I would also like to dedicate the book to them to remind us of a time when the sharing of our food and our stories became so important.

First published 2021

The History Press
97 St George's Place
Cheltenham, Gloucestershire, GL50 3QB
www.thehistorypress.co.uk
Text © Taffy Thomas MBE, 2021
Illustrations © Dotty Kultys, 2021

The right of Taffy Thomas MBE to be identified as the Author
of this work has been asserted in accordance with the
Copyright, Designs and Patents Act 1988.

British Library Cataloguing in Publication Data.
A catalogue record for this book is available from the British Library

ISBN 978 0 7509 9669 3

Typesetting and origination by Typo•glyphix
Printed and bound in Great Britain by TJ Books Ltd.

CONTENTS

PROLOGUE

Take your seat at the supper table, where we celebrate the place of food in folk tale and the place of the tale at the table. Welcome to a feast of both.

A WELCOME TOAST

A good meal
A good tale
And good company
Are all you need to merry be!

TT

ABOUT THE AUTHOR

Taffy Thomas has been living in the Lake District for more than forty years. He was founder of the legendary 1970s folk theatre company, Magic Lantern, which used shadow puppets and storytelling to illustrate folk tales. After surviving a major stroke in 1985, he used oral storytelling as speech therapy, which led to him finding a new career as a storyteller.

He set up the Storyteller's Garden and Tales in Trust, the Northern Centre for Storytelling, at Church Stile in Grasmere, Cumbria; he was asked to become a patron of the Society for Storytelling, and was awarded an MBE for services to storytelling and charity in the millennium honours list.

In January 2010 he was appointed the first UK Storyteller Laureate at the British Library. He was awarded the Gold Badge, the highest honour of the English Folk Dance and Song Society, that same year. At the 2013 British Awards for Storytelling Excellence (BASE), Taffy received the award for outstanding male storyteller and also the award for outstanding storytelling performance for his piece 'Ancestral Voices'.

More recently he has become a patron of Open Storytellers, a community arts charity supporting people with learning disabilities and autism; he is also patron of the East Anglian Storytelling Festival and of the South Lakeland Festival, Furness Traditions.

Taffy continues to tell stories and lead workshops, passing on both his skills and extensive repertoire. He is currently working on a new History Press book *Storytelling for Families*, to enable families to enjoy this precious art form together at home.

In 2020, while writing the manuscript for this book, his previous book *The Magpie's Nest: A Treasury of Bird Folk Tales* was winner of the Literature and Poetry category of the Lakeland Book of the Year awards.

ABOUT THE ILLUSTRATOR

Dotty Kultys directs, writes, designs and animates stories, experimenting with seemingly unfitting styles and focusing on characters that sometimes may get overlooked. With a BA in Acting and an MA in Animation, she specialises in directing, idea generation and character performance. In recent years she has worked on a variety of projects, ranging from book illustrations, narrative poetry and song lyrics, through studio work, to animated theatre projections, music videos and short films. She is currently working freelance in Bristol.

'When Taffy asked me to illustrate this collection of tales, I was thrilled. We've worked together before on animating one of his tales, "The Hunchback and the Swan", and it was an absolute delight. What better way to join forces again than by telling tales about food! I think it's particularly fitting that I'm illustrating this book just before Christmas. Yuletide is a time when my mum and I would spend entire evenings bustling about in the kitchen – sifting, grinding, cutting, mixing, kneading, forming, decorating – and all the while Mum would regale me with family tales, liberally sprinkling them with made-up silly rhymes. She probably doesn't realise this, but somewhere between dicing the prunes, singing a witty ditty, and tasting the borscht to check if it needed more pepper, she instilled in me an enduring love for making food and telling stories. Thank you, Mum, for this priceless gift – and thank you, Taffy, for this wonderful opportunity to celebrate it!'

FOREWORD

Sitting around a table and enjoying a good meal is a pleasure in itself. Eating in the company of a storyteller is an even greater pleasure. Imagine the idyllic atmosphere of such a supper, where, thanks to the story unfolding, the senses are heightened and the enjoyment of the narration mingles with that of the food until it forms a whole; a unique experience in which you can no longer tell if it's the body or the mind that is drawing comfort and sustenance from the meal.

With these happy associations of thoughts and images, I began to read the draft copy of the book that my dear friend Taffy had sent me, entrusting me with the pleasant task of providing some words of introduction.

From its first pages, *The Storyteller's Supper* immerses the reader in a world of folk tales and myths. These are stories that are capable of dealing with even the most complex of themes – always handled with a lightness of touch; so light in fact that it is barely detectible. Taffy is a master of this technique. He is one of those people whom I admire enormously because they have mastered something that has been praised since the days of Ovid. This is the art of simplicity – very rare in our times, though much needed.

And with the simplicity that proceeds from the language of everyday things, these stories are our companions for a meal that is rich in different flavours and which, course by course, teaches us some important values. As an example, I would like to share the beautiful message of hope embodied by the protagonists of 'Just Desserts', a couple for whom resources are scarce but whom I could never call poor. Throughout the story, thanks to the care they demonstrate towards all creation, living and non-living, they show great richness and goodness of spirit; virtues that in the end will turn out to be quite rewarding. This is just a small taste of what I'm sure you'll appreciate in the course of reading: a story that teaches the importance of humility of purpose, respect, and a sense of responsibility and community.

What makes this book really special, however, is its perspective on what food and folk stories have in common: their origin in tradition, whether cultural or oral; their sense of regionality; the very act of sharing; the presence of conviviality; and the celebration of diversity in all its forms. Taffy makes these connections by referencing the abundance of food in nature and through his understanding of dialects, popular traditions and in the details of everyday life. And if the uncertainty and frenzy of today's society results in a certain amount of both conformity and rootlessness, reading this book leads us instead to savour the many facets of life and rediscover our identity. Today, more than ever, humanity needs voices like Taffy's that preserve and bring to life these priceless traditions that form our cultural heritage and which are still very much part of us. This is the way to build a new pluralistic humanism that harnesses the full potential of diversity as an indispensable force for shaping our future.

So, until the moment when we can once more take our seat at the table and share the joy of a meal in the company of the people we love, I invite you to read and enjoy this wonderful book. While it may not be food for the body, it certainly offers nourishment and refreshment for the soul.

Long live storytellers; long live good food and culture that celebrates the beauty of diversity.

Happy reading!

Carlo Petrini
Founder of the global Slow Food movement
Listed in The Guardian's *100 people who can change the world*

INTRODUCTION

I love food; I never eat anything else! To some it is merely fuel – to others it is art.

Wherever you stand on this, it is undoubtedly part of our culture.

At the Storyteller's Supper both the stories and the food are celebrated as equal parts of our culture. At its simplest, the meal has to provide subsistence and comfort. A tale well-told can also provide subsistence to the imagination and can comfort the anxious. The full sensory experience of a meal can be savoured at the Storyteller's Supper, where the taste of the dish is further enhanced by the story of that dish and its ingredients. The storyteller can convey the magic of food history and the dish's journey to the table, hopefully with not too many food miles.

Many of the tales in this collection are about the pleasure of sharing food. My friend Norma Waterson once told me that her Irish grandmother always set an extra place at the table, never explaining this until Norma had grown up. Her grandmother then explained that the extra place was because 'you never know when you are eating with an angel!' Now that's a pleasing ghost story.

As with my previous History Press publications I have drawn the material from the canon of European folk tales and dishes, many from oral sources. As far as my ageing memory has allowed, I have acknowledged my sources in the introduction to each tale. Whilst I am equally enthusiastic about world tales and food culture, that's another book for another day. However, I have included a couple of tales from the Far East that proved irresistible to me. These I have respectfully reworked, making them placeless and timeless so I can comfortably tell them in my own voice. In short, I have used their bones, but not their flesh, believing the only way you can harm a folk tale is by not telling it.

Without the support of The History Press team you wouldn't have this book in your hands. Also, without the support of my wife Chrissy this collection would never have come together and I would possibly have starved to death working on it! As it happens, if I can cook, it is because back in the 1960s a group of us lads from Yeovil Grammar School set out weekly, clutching a basket of ingredients and our aprons, to the high school for girls, where the domestic science teacher, Miss Pink, taught us to cook. Although as teenagers our motivation wasn't solely culinary, we did return home with supper for our families in our baskets. Parents and siblings dutifully ate it.

Pondering this collection, I think of all those who have ever told me a story or fed me. Many of these are long gone and now only live in my mind as ancestral voices. Dialect stories are also included, as I have always understood the importance of regional dialect to be what the late Charles Parker called 'the poetry of the common man'. My Somerset dialect tale draws on my memory of my mother's and my grandfather's voices when I listened to them on their Somerset farm. The Westmorland dialect tale from my friend, Edward Acland, draws on his memory of the voice of his grandfather. Given the roots of these tales it is a fact that, like my ingredients, they have travelled directly from field to table.

My wish is that this book will encourage us to grow or shop well, to cook well, to eat well and to listen well as we cling on to this spinning globe. As this fits in well with the aspirations of the 'Slow Food' movement I feel honoured that my Italian friend of many years, Carlo Petrini, the founder of this global movement, has graced these pages with a foreword. I am also delighted that Polish film animator and illustrator Dotty Kultys animates these pages with such tasty illustrations. If these and the tales feed your imagination maybe you will even set up your own Storyteller's Supper.

Taffy Thomas
The Storyteller's House, Ambleside 2020

from
field
and
furrow

Part I

FROM FIELD & FURROW

Oats and beans and barley grow
As you and I and everyone know
First the farmer sows the seed
Then he stands to take his ease
Stamps his feet and claps his hands
And turns around to view his land
Oats and beans and barley grow
As you and I and everyone know

Jack and the Boggart

*Throughout these islands there are magical tales of mischievous
little creatures. Variously named imps, sprites, boggles, boggarts,
piskies, leprechauns, hobs or elves, they wreak havoc in the lives
of ordinary folk.*

*Every good tale needs a hero, and Jack, not too bright and
not over fond of work, is often the lad to deal with these ne'er-
do-wells, tricksters or even a boggart who has pitched up on
his farm. This story tells of how Jack outwitted this bothersome
boggart and managed to save his precious harvest in order to
ensure that his family could have a loaf of freshly baked bread
each day.*

Jack lived on his family farm in the north-west of England.
He lived with his father, who had inherited the farm from his

father, who had in turn inherited it from his father and so on, back to the days of the Doomsday Book. It was natural that when Jack's father died peacefully one night, full of years, that his only son Jack would take over the farm.

The day after the funeral, when Jack rose early shaking himself ready for work, a boggart took up residence in the ditch at the bottom of the fifteen-acre field. Jack only discovered this when his pair of shire horses ploughed a furrow clean and straight the length of the field. When he made a big turn, lining up for a second furrow, he saw that his first furrow had been filled in ... and not neatly! There on the edge of the ditch, mocking Jack, stood the boggart, hooting with laughter. Jack told the boggart that it should clear off as it was trespassing on his land. The boggart retorted that its family had made their home in that ditch for generations so he had every right to be there and would not budge. Jack told him that couldn't be true as neither he nor any of his family had ever set eyes on any of them.

The boggart told him that all boggarts keep themselves to themselves, sleeping both day and night. This admission of laziness gave clever Jack an idea. He told the boggart that if it let him get on with his work he would give half of all his crops to it and it could then just sleep the days away. Not surprisingly, the boggart agreed to this offer.

For their first crop, Jack asked the boggart if it wanted 'tops' or 'bottoms'. When it decided 'tops', Jack planted a field of beetroot. When the beets were harvested Jack got baskets of the delicious purple roots and the boggart only a crop of bitter leaves.

For the next crop the boggart insisted on 'bottoms', so clever Jack planted a field of cauliflowers. When these were harvested Jack got baskets of cream and green caulis the size of footballs and the boggart just bitter stalks and wormy roots.

The boggart, who had become increasingly angry, told Jack that the next crop had to be wheat, and that the field should be divided across the middle by a rope. Then it would have the bottom half and Jack could have the top half. Jack agreed to this and immediately started ploughing and harrowing the field. He then set about sowing wheat seeds using a seed fiddle, a box of seeds strapped to his back with a wheel and a bow like a violin bow at the bottom. As Jack walked up and down the field he fiddled the bow backwards and forwards and this turned the wheel, shooting seeds out in each direction. He then stretched a rope across the middle of the field, dividing it in half.

Having prepared the field Jack then made his way to the blacksmith's forge with a strange request. He asked the smith to make a couple of dozen fake metal wheat stalks and paint them yellow. Jack then waited for the sun and rain to do their work. It wasn't long before tiny green shots started to appear in the fifteen-acre field. As soon as these stalks started to ripen and turn golden, Jack took the fake metal wheat stalks and planted them among the golden wheat stalks in the boggart's half of the field. Jack then woke the boggart in his ditch and told it that it was time to harvest. The boggart sharpened his scythe and, swinging it, set off up the field. It had only gone but fifty yards when there was a clang as the scythe blade hit a metal stalk and shattered. The boggart had to head to the blacksmith's for a new blade. With the scythe repaired, it continued its reaping but only got another fifty yards before 'clang!' another ruined scythe blade. After another visit to the blacksmith, who, pleased with the trade coming his way, had mended the blade immediately, the boggart had one more attempt at harvesting the wheat when, 'clang!' the same thing happened.

Exasperated by this thankless task, the boggart gave up, telling Jack he was welcome to the field and its useless crops and that he had decided to leave the area for fresh fields. Jack waited to make sure the boggart had flitted before coiling up the rope and collecting the metal stalks; they had done their job.

The following day was fine. Jack sharpened his scythe and harvested the whole field. He then fixed the sheaves of wheat on his cart and took them to the miller. As he watched the mill wheel turning he knew he'd be taking home many sacks of freshly milled flour. This meant that for many weeks following, his cottage would be filled with the satisfying smell of freshly baked bread.

The Wheat Flower

I have long collected riddle tales but this tale has joined my repertoire since the publication of my Riddle in the Tale *book and finds itself in this new collection. It leads beautifully into a poem gifted to me on my 70th birthday by friend and storyteller Shonaleigh. It was written by her mother, Edith Marks. I thank them both. The motifs within the story of riddles and the value of the wisdom of elders recur in many folk tales throughout the world. This version has its roots in Eastern Europe.*

Before my time and before your time, but in somebody's time, there was a cantankerous old king. Despite the fact that he had an heir in the shape of his only son who was both keen and bright, the king clung on to power, like a magnet to a piece of iron. The prince, with his youthful enthusiasm, became increasingly frustrated. The idea that the dreams and energy of young people like himself were crushed by the stubbornness of old men so grew in his mind that he vowed that as soon as he felt the weight of the crown on his head he would banish all old people from his kingdom on pain of death.

Despite the old king clinging on to life and power, eventually and inevitably the grim reaper did pay a call. The prince felt both sadness and relief as a state funeral led to his crowning. With the weight of the crown came the weight of responsibility and he wondered why he had been so keen for this moment to come. Collecting himself and his energies, he proclaimed his intent to free the young folk and allow their dreams to take flight. Every family was ordered to banish their elders on pain of death if they disobeyed. Soon down the road stretched a trail of ancient refugees, many stumbling, some with sticks or crutches. What a dismal sight!

There was, however, in one corner of the kingdom, a young farmer who was both brave and wise. He had been taught all he knew about farming and life by his elderly grandfather. There was no way they were prepared to be parted. The old man was hidden away in a large wooden barrel in the corner of the barn. Soon when soldiers came searching for any families disobeying the king's orders, the young farmer gave them free strong beer to distract them. More than a little drunk, the soldiers didn't notice the wooden barrel, and the old man and his grandson remained unharmed. As far as the new king was concerned, his orders had been obeyed by everyone. He could now choose to take a wife, a princess who soon bore him a beautiful daughter. But things did not go well for the young king and his people. With all the knowledge and experience of the wise elders gone, when people, their animals or crops were ailing, nobody had the experience to put them right. Medicine, horticulture and husbandry rely on the knowledge accrued over generations.

Time passed, and just when the king thought things couldn't get worse, they did. The time had come for him to choose the most suitable husband for his daughter. Wanting to find someone who could match the girl in wit and intellect, he decided every young man in the kingdom would have three riddles to solve in order to gain her hand. The princess, who had the passion and verve her father had once had, wasn't too happy with this method of choosing a husband, but dutifully accepted it.

The following day there was a line of suitors at the castle gates. At the very end of the line was our young farmer, with little hope for his chances. The king told them that to be successful they would have to solve three riddles. For the first riddle the king told the suitors that he wanted them to return the following morning bringing him a rope woven from ashes. The farmer rushed back to tell his wise old grandfather of the task he had been set and to seek his help. Peering out of the barrel, the old man smiled, advising his grandson to weave a rope very, very tight, place it on a tin tray then burn it slowly. And then at daybreak he should carefully carry the tray with the rope of ashes to the castle. The next morning the young farmer followed his grandfather's advice. All of the other suitors had started with piles of ash and tried to weave or mould it, with no success. So they only arrived with dirty hands and wheelbarrows full of ash. To the amazement of everyone there, when the young farmer arrived he 'cut a dash', bearing a tray with a perfectly formed rope of ashes. Amazed, the king announced him the winner. The princess just smiled in admiration. One riddle down, two to go.

This time the suitors were instructed to return the following day wearing boots, but barefoot! Again the farmer returned to seek the advice of his grandfather. With his head and arms free of the barrel the old man told his grandson to bring a pair of boots and a pair of shears. The old man cut the uppers from the soles. When the young farmer put them on he was wearing the boots but his feet were touching the ground. Arriving at the castle, most of the suitors were either in their stocking feet, or wearing one shoe on and one shoe off. The king asked the farmer why he was still wearing his normal boots and the young man lifted his feet to reveal the pink soles. The king again declared him the winner. Two riddles down, one riddle to go.

For the final task, each suitor had to court the princess by bringing her the most beautiful flower they could find. Again the wise old man in the barrel aided his grandson. Arriving at the castle, the farmer joined a queue of men all with armfuls of roses, lilies and orchids. At the end of the line was the young farmer bearing a simple golden, ripe wheat stalk. On seeing this, the princess appeared both surprised and insulted in equal measure. The farmer told her that he thought that a field of golden wheat rippling in a summer breeze was as beautiful as any exotic bloom, and once harvested and the flour baked into bread the smell from the kitchen was as enticing as the scent of any flower. Smiling and excited, the princess jumped up and down. The king smiled gently, realising that the young man had indeed captured the heart and hand of his daughter. He couldn't resist asking the young farmer where the wisdom to answer these riddles had come from. The farmer now felt confident enough to tell the king of his grandfather hidden in the barn. The king, realising the farmer had so much respect for his grandfather he was prepared to risk his life for him, became aware that he would soon grow old and wish to be likewise respected by his daughter and his subjects. He forgave the farmer his disobedience and decreed that all of the families of the kingdom should bring home their old folk and their wisdom to enrich and benefit the future of the kingdom. And so it was that the kingdom blossomed!

From that day, whenever the smell of freshly baked bread drifted out from any house in that kingdom, folk remembered the special 'flower' that was a gift to the princess.

> When you are hungry,
> Make bread and give it to the hungry.
> When you are lonely,
> Make bread and give it to the lonely.
> When you are sad,
> Make bread and give it to those full of sorrow.
> When you are frustrated,
> Make bread. Take time to knead it well
> And share it with the frustrated.
> When you are happy,
> Make bread and share it with those
> Who are also happy.
> When you are victorious,
> Make bread and give it to your enemy.
> When you have no flour,

Sit and tell the story of all the times
You made bread and shared it.
But first –
Learn to make bread!

Edith Marks

A Baker for the Fairies

In many of the Celtic stories about fairies, they are called the 'good people'. In several of the tales in my repertoire the fairies are anything but good, being not averse to kidnapping a traveller or anyone who would stray too near their 'fairy forts'. My main source of information about fairy lore goes back to time spent with Irish piper and storyteller Seamus Ennis. You might almost forgive the fairy folk if their kidnap victim was the finest baker in the land who could provide them with the sweetmeats they craved. Even in this Scottish tale I have managed to sneak in a bit of fairy lore from Seamus in order to protect my 'baker' readers, especially my granddaughter, Ona, who is both an avid story reader and an enthusiastic baker. Indeed she 'road-tested' the fairy cakes recipe for the Storyteller's Supper menu.

In the highlands of Scotland there once was a tiny croft that was home to a woman who was the finest baker in the land. Her macaroons melted in the mouth, her flapjacks were a meal in themselves and her rock buns, though hard on the crust, were butter-kissed soft in the centre. This woman was not only a wonderful baker, she was also honest and kind. Any of the villagers who ordered cakes from her were charged a fair price, but if any of the poorer folk needed something to sweeten their lives the chances are that an elaborate cake bejewelled with cherries would arrive at their door as a gift.

Now it just happened that on the other side of the hamlet stood a strange hill. This was a hollow hill, a fairy fort, home to a colony of the fairy folk, and fairies as we know often have a sweet tooth. These tiny folk would creep into people's houses to steal a piece of cake or even to scoff their leftover crumbs. It annoyed the fairy folk greatly that whenever they visited the baker's kitchen, or the house of anyone she supplied, there was never so much as a single crumb to steal as her bakes were so mouth-watering that every last morsel had been gobbled up. These hungry fairies realised that the only way that they could enjoy the baker's fare was to kidnap her and take her back to their fairy fort to bake cakes just for them. But how to capture her?

Their chance came sooner than they expected. It just happened that the daughter of the laird who lived in a big house nearby was about to be married. Of course, the laird only wanted the best for his daughter, so he arranged for our baker to make all the cakes for the feast, including the towering wedding cake. In her little croft the baker set to work for this was her most important job of the year ... Or so she thought! She packed her goodies into a large handcart to make her delivery to the big house. Her husband couldn't help her to go and set up as he had to stay home to care for their baby and cat and dog. He had, however, heard of the little people, and knowing of the superstitions of country folk, advised his wife to wear her coat inside out to avoid being fairy-led. The trouble was that the baker was so hot from doing all that baking she had no intention of wearing any coat any way out; and wasn't it hot midsummer anyway?

Pushing the cart of cakes, the baker set off for the laird's house. Some way down the road she passed a mulberry bush, where the fairy folk were hiding to spot their victim and make a plan to kidnap her on her way home. As she approached the big house, she heard the sound of the piper playing and the whooping as the family and guests danced the Gay Gordons to the tune of 'Haste to the Wedding'. She took great pains to lay out the array of cakes beautifully on the banquet table and assemble the towering wedding cake in pride of place at the centre. She then set out back down the road home. As she neared the mulberry bush, the fairies flew out, circling her head and confusing her beyond reason. She thought the wings brushing against her face were those of moths or fireflies and dropped down on to a mossy bank. Collecting herself and struggling to her feet, she discovered that she was being led through a crack in the nearby hill. She was now a prisoner in the fairy fort.

She assured the cluster of fairies crowding around her that her husband would pay a ransom as his love for her was even greater than his love for her baking! The fairies replied that no ransom was necessary as it was indeed her baking skills that they required. She was thinking that she had no intention of remaining a prisoner in a fairy fort for long but she did not mind doing some baking, and asked to be shown around their kitchen. On searching for a mixing bowl, she discovered that, being tiny folk, their mixing bowl was only the size of an eggcup, and that would never do. A couple of fairies were dispatched to her croft to fetch her much larger bowl. As soon as they returned with the bowl, the woman, having discovered that all their spoons were even smaller than teaspoons, sent them back for her large wooden spoons and spatulas. Arriving back with these and now becoming a little fed up, they were sent back again for the baker's balloon whisk. A couple more fairies were also sent for flour and milk. As soon as they returned, they were sent off again for eggs and sugar. By now all the fairies were a bit weary and annoyed at continually being sent back and forth on errands. The woman set to work measuring and mixing. Somehow the batter would not come right. She told the fairies that when she made her best buns her cat was usually purring at her feet and she would mix to the rhythm of the purring. A fairy was sent to the croft to collect the cat, a ginger tom. The sharp claws of the cat dug into the fairy's arm and made the fairy even grumpier. Once at the feet of the woman, the cat settled down to purring and she continued with the beating of the batter to the rhythm of the cat's purring. She told the fairies that the mix still wasn't quite right and that usually on a baking day her dog had pride of place in the kitchen. Another fairy was sent to the croft to collect the dog. The dog, not liking being taken from the cosiness of its basket, bit the fairy who, now more annoyed than ever, quickly delivered the dog to its owner. As the woman greased the cake trays, she remembered her husband and baby and told the fairies that the success of her baking relied on them being there to make her feel at home. Long-suffering fairies were sent to collect them.

Arriving at the fairy fort and surveying the scene, the husband felt relieved. Now he realised why his wife had disappeared and also why various things had mysteriously vanished from the kitchen. He was confident that his wife was not just clever in the kitchen but was also clever enough to have hatched a plan to enable them all to escape back to the safety of their croft. He wasn't wrong!

The woman knew that as much as fairies love sweet things, they hate loud noise. She handed her husband a wooden spoon and whispered to him to prod the dog. He prodded the dog with the spoon, not too hard though, and the dog began to bark.

At this the baby began to cry and the fairies, wincing, used their wings to block their ears. The husband, guessing his wife's plan, gently trod on the cat's tail. The cat yowled out, increasing the racket even more. The fairies, who could not bear this hullabaloo, marched the husband holding the baby, the cat and the dog out of the side of the hill, pointing them down the road with instructions for them not to return. The woman, trying to follow them, was told she would have to stay until she had completed her baking task. She told the fairies that the cakes would turn out much better if they were baked in her croft on the cooking range that she was well used to using. If they agreed to let her go home she would cook them special fairy cakes every week and leave them on the flat granite stone by the entrance to their fairy fort. The fairies were happy with this and, fancying some peace and quiet after all of their errands, agreed.

The woman kept her word, and to her delight, whenever she left a plate of her cakes on the rock, as soon as they disappeared they were replaced by a small bag of fairy gold … payment indeed. Mind you, she never again set off on her deliveries down the road past the fairy fort without wearing her coat inside out.

The Rice Stone

Rice is one of the great staples in the diet of many cultures. For communities living in the East, rice is grown in the paddy fields. Europe, however, has its own culture of rice-based dishes where wetlands have been created near rivers to enable its growth. The short-grained Spanish rice is grown to make paella, a delicious dish that features in the following tale.

This charming Spanish story was recorded from Felissa Vivas, an old lady from Extremadura, in 1988. It was translated and gifted to me by my friend, storyteller John Pole. The tale contains three of the motifs often found in European folk tales: a magic pot, a magic stone and the surprise contents of a fish's stomach! It is a tale I was keen to collect, knowing my bilingual granddaughters would love it. Hope you do too.

A small man called Uncle Antonio lived with his dog, his only companion, in a small house in a town in southern Spain. This little town had spread itself over both sides of a river … and there was no bridge. Even though Uncle Antonio was very poor, he would go without food rather than see his little dog hungry. One day, however, things got so bad that as he sat down at the table to eat, with the dog at his feet, he told the dog that this might be their last meal. After this he knew they would have to starve to death or whatever God decided. As he was giving the dog this sad news there was a knock at the door.

It was a starving tramp begging for food. Although Antonio told the man that they were in a sorry state and having the last food they had, the tramp pushed open the door and walked in. The tramp said nothing but without a 'by your leave' he sat at the table. He grabbed a spoon and fork and gobbled up all of their dinner. The dog growled in disbelief and Antonio told him that now they would surely starve sooner than they had thought.

The tramp told them that he had no money to give to make up for what he had done, but that he could give the only thing he had, a white stone. What good would that be? The tramp told Antonio that if he put a pot of water to boil and dropped the white stone in then they would never run out of rice. Antonio and the dog doubted this, but had nothing left to lose. They put a pot of water on to boil and dropped the stone in. The tramp disappeared out of the door as quickly as he had come without them even noticing. Then Antonio and the dog settled down for their usual siesta. They were woken up by a glorious smell filling their kitchen. The pot was full, not just with rice, but with delicious paella more fragrant and tasty than any in the whole of Spain. They ate better than they ever had before. When the pot was empty they filled it up with water once more. As the pot cooked, it filled with paella again. The aroma drifted out of the window, catching the nostrils of a wandering scrawny cat. The cat made its way to Antonio's door and now there was enough rice for the kind uncle to feed it as well. Even the dog didn't seem to mind ... but that was to change.

Uncle Antonio's fortunes had changed. There was enough paella for folk to visit with their bowls and buy rice for a few coins. Antonio and the dog were no longer poor. Then one day, as Antonio filled the pot with water, he noticed that the white stone was missing. Without it, all he had was a pot of boiling water. He told the dog what had happened and together they searched the house from top to bottom, but there was no sign of the stone. Then Antonio realised that when one of the villagers had come with a bowl to buy paella he must have dished up the white stone with the rice. Who should return at that moment but the hungry cat. When the dog told the cat about the missing stone the two animals decided to search every house in town to find it. The skinny cat could get into any house, especially in the summer when at least one window would be open. The unlikely pair made a call to every house on that side of the river. While the dog waited by the door, the cat slunk through an open window to search the house but had no luck. The pair of them decided that they would need to search the houses on the far side of the river.

With no bridge to cross, the dog, knowing he could swim well, told the cat to balance on his back. Excitedly the cat jumped on and the two unlikely friends managed to get to the other side of the river. Again they began their search at the first two houses without luck. Then in the third house the cat crept out and in her mouth was the white stone. Now they could take it back to Uncle Antonio.

As the dog started swimming home with the cat on his back the cat became so excited looking around at the view from on high that she spluttered and the stone plopped into the water. When they reached the bank at the other side, the cat had to admit to the dog that she had dropped the precious white stone in the middle of the river. The dog told the cat that he would certainly make her pay for this. On hearing this she turned tail and ran for her life.

Every day after this the dog went down to the river to try and spot the stone, but without luck. The local fishermen, seeing the friendly dog every day, became fond of him and would sometimes give him a fish, which he took home to

Uncle for their supper. One day the men were pleased at catching some really big fish and happily gave the dog one of them. Delighted, Antonio cut the fish open and believe it or not, inside the fish's stomach was the white stone. The stone was quickly washed and placed in the pot of water and indeed it filled up with the fragrant rice. The magic still worked. For supper that night Uncle Antonio and the dog again dined well. Then, would you believe it, the cat had the nerve to peep through the open door and try her luck. The dog made a face at her, growled, barked and chased her away. Ever since that day, that is the way of it with dogs and cats. The folk of Spain, however, to this day enjoy sharing the beautiful, fragrant, rice dish of paella together.

Strawberry Porridge

The motif of a pot that magically fills with goodies recurs in folk tales. In the 'Rice Stone' story in this collection the pot fills magically with rice but in the story that follows a pot magically fills with oats. Oats have been a staple in the north of Britain, where the climate makes it less suitable for growing wheat or barley. Viking invaders knew this crop and called it 'Haver'. Because of this, the bag used to carry oats became a haversack. Apart from this, where would we be in colder weather without porridge? On a good day mine comes topped with a wee dram, 'Royal porridge'. Well my Lakeland home is part of the 'Debatable' lands, the ancient border with Scotland!

There was once a girl whose father and mother had sadly died when she was young, so she went to live with her grandmother in a tiny cottage at the top of a hill above the village. At the back of the cottage was a forest. In winter the young girl went there with her grandmother to collect firewood. Although she was young, she was strong and wanted to help her grandmother with the carrying. On these outings the old woman would point to plants on the ground with tiny white flowers, telling the girl that the flowers would soon be replaced by wild strawberries. The berries would first appear green before turning white and then bright red. As soon as the berries turned red it could be the young girl's job to take a basket and pick them to bring home.

When her grandmother told her that the day had come when the strawberries might be right for picking, the girl took a basket and set off to collect the berries. Her grandmother had given her a crust of fresh bread to enjoy, as being in the fresh air picking the berries might make her feel hungry. When her basket was full the girl sat down for a rest and, taking the crust of bread from her pocket, began to eat. It was then that she noticed a crooked stick and a pair of battered boots next to her. Looking upwards, she saw the bony shape of a beggar woman. The stranger told her that she was also in the forest to pick the wild strawberries as she had no other food and had not tasted even a crust of bread for a week. Selflessly the young girl held out the remains of her crust of bread to the starving woman, who ate it gratefully as one who hasn't seen a loaf of bread for many days. The beggar woman thanked the girl, telling her that she had shown such kindness to her she'd like to give her something in return. The only thing she had with her was the pot she brought to carry the strawberries, so she handed it to the girl. She told her that if she put the pot on the kitchen table and said, 'Little pot, little pot, make me porridge,' then it would magically fill with delicious steaming hot porridge, but when the pot was full she must say, 'Little pot, little pot, enough!' and it would stop. The young girl wasn't sure whether to believe her but politely thanked her for the gift. Starting for home with her basket of berries and the pot, the girl turned to wave to the beggar woman, only to find that she had disappeared to 'who knows where'.

Her grandmother was pleased to see her back with the berries. When she told her grandmother that she had given away her crust of bread to a beggar woman, and that the woman had given her a pot in return, the grandmother wasn't sure. However, when the girl put the pot on the kitchen table and said, 'Little pot, little pot make me porridge,' and the pot started to fill with delicious steaming porridge, her grandmother was more impressed. She took a bowl and spooned some of the porridge into it and bejewelled it with the lovely red strawberries as the pot filled to the top. She was so pleased with the porridge that she didn't hear the girl say, 'Little pot, little pot, enough!' to make the pot stop. Filling up another bowlful, the two settled down to a fine breakfast of strawberry porridge.

Now it so happened that in the loft the grandmother kept chickens. Once a week the young girl would collect the eggs in a basket and take them to the market to sell or barter for bread and vegetables. The very next day was market day so the girl collected the eggs and, saying she wouldn't be too long, she headed off to market, telling her grandmother that they could have more of the delicious porridge on her return. It took longer than usual to sell all of the eggs that day and by the afternoon she still hadn't returned. But wasn't the old grandmother getting hungry! The thought of the strawberry porridge that was to come made her mouth water. She couldn't resist placing the pot on the kitchen table and, when she repeated the young girl's words, 'Little pot, little pot, make me porridge', sure enough the pot began to fill with porridge.

As soon as it was half full, the grandmother realised that she would need a bowl and a spoon, and while she went to the pantry to fetch them, the pot continued to make porridge. Soon the pot was full and the porridge was pouring over the top of it, into the grandmother's lap and over the edge of the table. She tried to cover the pot, but that didn't work. She begged it to stop but that didn't work either. She started to cry at her bad luck, but by now the room was filling with porridge. As it was summer the cottage door was open and the porridge was soon streaming out of the door and down the hill towards the village. All the grandmother could do was to go up to the loft and then on to the roof with her chickens, lamenting her misfortune. She wished for the young girl's return but that didn't happen … well not for a while anyway.

The squire, struggling up the hill to his big house, was soon up to his gaiters in porridge. The vicar on his bicycle was soon cycling through a sticky stream of porridge and fell off. In the market square the young girl saw the river of porridge flowing down the hill and guessed what had happened. If only her grandmother had waited for her to get home. She struggled up the hill, making her way through the sticky stream, and as soon as she reached the cottage she shouted, 'Little pot, little pot, enough.' To the grandmother's relief, the pot immediately stopped and the young girl called her grandmother down from the roof. Together they cleared up the gooey mess and decided that after all that had happened they would wait until breakfast the following day before using the porridge pot again. Peering out of the window, they even managed a smile as they watched the farm workers and market traders, at the end of their working day, having to eat their way home!

As Good as Gold

We storytellers are 'magpies', adding to our repertoire with every journey we make. Collecting these tales is, at best, an informal affair between new friends over a table of food and drink. The stories travel from the ear to the mouth and the memory.

In the 1970s and '80s I made many new Dutch friends at Sidmouth International Folk Festival and folk camps in Holland. With these fond memories I am delighted to have found a Dutch tale for this collection, my version of the Lady of Stavoren.

The tale comes from a land that was historically a great maritime trading nation. Although it imported many exotic ingredients from the Far East to Western Europe, this tale concerns a staple ingredient that we learn can be 'as good as gold'.

The town of Stavoren stands on the northern coast of Holland in the province of Friesland. In the days of merchant sailing ships it was a wealthy port, having a large harbour perfectly placed for great merchant ships to join the North Sea before heading east to the Scandinavian countries or north and south across the Atlantic to the Americas, the Indies and Holland's great trading nations in the Middle and Far East. It was not surprising that with such wealth Stavoren boasted a community of rich merchants living in grand houses who liked to exhibit their riches whenever possible. Many of them even had accoutrements of real gold adorning the entrances to their homes. However, as is the way to this day, a community of poor folk lived next to the mansions of the rich and successful. Most of these rich merchants knew the price of everything and the value of nothing. However, there was one elderly merchant who was not quite so crass. If poor folk arrived at his door he would send his servants to prepare a basket of food to help them, for after all didn't he and his wife have plenty to spare? This kind merchant's wife, however, danced to a different tune. She viewed her husband's kind nature as weakness and if she answered the door to poor beggars they would be sent packing.

In time the kind old merchant died and his estate passed to his mean-natured wife. This estate included their mansion house, its staff, and a small fleet of trading ships complete with their captains and crews. As much as she enjoyed being the envy of all of the townsfolk, this did not satisfy her vanity. Although she had the finest house in the town and gold and silver in store, she wanted to own the most precious thing in the world, and in truth she had no idea what this might be. She called her sea captains together for a meeting. Now most of these captains were old 'salts' who had grown up in sea-faring families around the dock, and they looked admiringly at the merchant houses decorated with gold surrounding the harbour. There was one captain, however, who was different. He had been brought up on a farm in the middle of Friesland before making his way to the sea port seeking adventure, and by hard work had made his way up from cabin boy to captain. Growing up on a farm, the only gold he had ever seen was the gold of the fields of corn.

The vainglorious widow instructed her captains to set sail and only return when they had filled her ships with the most precious thing in the world. The first captain set his course for Africa and after several months returned with a cargo of carved ivory. While this pleased the lady, she was curious to know if her other ships would return with something even better. The second captain set his course for the Far East and returned some time later with a ship filled with fine silks, pearls and exquisite pottery. The widow thought this a little better, but still wondered if the most precious thing in the world was still to come. The sea captain who had been brought up on the land could not decide in which direction to head, but he had to try. Setting sail a few months later, he chanced to dock in a port on the Baltic coast. Heading ashore, on the quayside the captain spotted a large wooden store with its huge doors spread wide open. There seemed to be a golden glow shining out from inside the store, a sharp contrast to the constant blue and grey of the sea and sky that had filled his eyes for so long. He was drawn towards the golden glow and discovered that the huge building was a granary filled to the rooftop with wheat. The sight and smell reminded the captain of his childhood spent on the farm. Thinking that some of that wheat may even have come from his homeland, he remembered all the beautiful bread that had been baked from flour ground from the wheat of those fields. Surely this must be the most precious thing in the world? Believing this, he purchased the whole contents of the huge granary. Summoning his crew, he ordered them to set to work filling the entire ship with the wheat, and set sail back to Stavoren.

A year and a day had passed and word had spread around the town that the last of the widow's ships was due to dock on the next tide. All the townsfolk rushed to the dockside and the widow arrived dressed, of course, in her finery. The sea captain strode down the gangplank and bowed to his employer. The lady, as ever lacking in grace, only wanted to know what cargo he had returned with. Had he managed to bring her the most precious thing in the world? When he told her that he had brought her a ship full of golden wheat the lady turned white with shock before quickly turning red with fury. She told the captain that wheat was common and that she had no place in her life for common. She ordered him to empty all the wheat into the harbour and sail away. The captain told her that this would be a criminal act as there were many people in the town for whom wheat would be a lifesaver if turned into flour and bread. The lady merely retorted that poor folk, wheat, flour and indeed bread were common and that she had no place in her life for common. The captain fixed her with a meaningful eye, telling her that the day might come when she herself was poor and in need of bread. This was an insult too much and the lady tore a large expensive ring from her finger, tossing it far out to sea and proclaiming that the ring would return to her finger before she was ever poor. The crowd gathered even closer to enjoy the drama. Again the lady ordered the captain to empty the wheat into the harbour and sail away. Sadly the captain turned his back on the lady and the townsfolk and climbed back on board, ordering his crew to cast off. As the ship sailed out of the harbour the entire cargo of wheat was consigned to the depths of the sea near the harbour entrance.

As the lady made her way back to her mansion, she passed a group of fishermen who had just returned with their catch. Deciding that she would improve her day by asking her cook to prepare her favourite meal of fish baked with fresh herbs and butter, she purchased a fine-looking fish and told the fisherman to deliver it to her kitchen. Arriving home she called for the cook and instructed him to prepare the fish for supper. That evening the cook served the fish on a silver plate to the lady and as he cut the fillet from the bone the lady spotted something glittering in the middle of the fish. Yes, there was the very ring that she had cast into the sea! As she washed it clean in her glass of fine wine before replacing it on her finger, she wondered. The memory of the sea captain's warning of possible ill fortune reared up in her memory.

'As sure as eggs are eggs,' things started to go wrong for the lady. Week by week news came of each of her ships floundering and sinking in great storms at sea with the loss of her cargoes and with them her wealth. After a year all the folk of Stavoren were amazed to see a green barrier growing out of the water at the harbour entrance. All of the wheat cast into the sea had sprouted and grown. This barrier obstructed the free flowing of the tides in and out of the harbour. The docks silted up. This prevented large merchant ships making Stavoren their destination or port of departure. Trade plummeted and Stavoren went from being a great trading port to being a small town on the Friesland coast used for the arrival and departure of a small ferry. Most of the merchants who had been obscenely wealthy had to settle for a much simpler life, having more in common with the poorer folk of the town. As for the widow, all she had done was to secure her place in history. She did this through the survival of this tale and the fact that the sand bar at the harbour entrance is still called 'The Lady's Sand'. Her reward for pouring scorn on the most precious 'gold' in the world? Wheat!

The Golden Harp, 'Y Delyn Aur'

My father was born in the Merthyr Vale, so it's great to include a folk tale from 'the Land of my Fathers'. It was my delight most weekends to visit my grandparents at their railway cottage. Although there was a cooker in their little kitchen, on autumn and winter days the seriously tasty delights came from the fireplace in the living room. The bake stone (pronounced back stone) was fetched from the cupboard and placed on the coals until glowing red hot. Then Grandma Thomas would set to, making Welsh cakes. After being flipped, they were dredged with caster sugar and eaten warm. What's not to like about that?

The town of Dolgellau lies at the foot of Cader Idris, the legendary 'Chair of Idris'. As you start to climb this mountain, you will pass a terrace of well-kept cottages. The end cottage of this terrace was once a musical house, the home of Morgan Preece and his wife Anna. Anna's fingers could dance lightly across the strings of her harp and she had the voice of an angel. Morgan, her husband, was a kind man but no musician. He had a voice like a crow and fingers like thumbs.

One day Anna had gone down into town to join in a musical gathering, a 'Noson Lawen', and as Morgan sat alone in his grandfather chair by the fire there was a knock on the door. Morgan opened the door to discover three strangers standing there. He was not to know that they were some of the fairy folk who lived among the rocks and caves a little farther up the mountain come to test the welcome Morgan and Anna gave to their kind in their home. The fairy folk were welcomed in most of the cottages and in return for a warm welcome would often bestow gifts on their hosts. The spokesman for the three strangers told Morgan that they were hungry and thirsty and in need of a little rest. No one came to the home of Morgan and Anna and left hungry! He settled his visitors at the table and disappeared into the pantry, returning with three mugs of ale and some Welsh cakes from the tin that Anna refilled weekly. Anna was famous for her Welsh cakes, which she cooked on the bake stone over the fire. The three strangers thanked Morgan warmly and began to eat and drink but he was surprised to notice that they sat in silence as they did so. Then, on finishing the last mouthful, the spokesman suddenly jumped up and declared that Anna's Welsh cakes were the best they had ever come across in the whole of Dolgellau. They all agreed and asked Morgan what they could give him in exchange for his welcome hospitality. Morgan told them he was a happy man who wanted for nothing except the gift of music. Heading for the door, the three told him that his wish would be granted.

A minute or so later there was a flash of light and a puff of smoke causing Morgan to exclaim '*Bobol Bach!*' As the smoke cleared Morgan was amazed to see in the corner of the room there stood a golden harp, 'Y Delyn Aur', studded with red and green jewels. Only then did Morgan realise that he had been entertaining the fairy folk. Walking over to the harp, he placed his fingers on the strings, knowing he had not the skill to play it. As he drew his fingers across the strings, the most beautiful music came forth from the magic harp.

The family next door heard the sweet music, and having seen Anna the musician leave for town that morning, called round to investigate. As they entered the living room to see Morgan sitting at the harp, they started to laugh and then to dance. As long as Morgan played they couldn't seem to stop dancing, even if their sides began to ache.

When Morgan eventually stopped playing in order to tell them of his magical visitors, they thankfully drew breath and sat down to listen. This family were the friendly neighbours. At the far end of the terrace was the home of Evan Jones, who was known as 'Jones the Sneer', never such a welcome visitor. He only called to torment or make trouble. When he 'put the knife in' it twisted. By now rumours of Morgan's musical prowess had reached his ears and he couldn't resist calling to spoil Morgan's happiness. He told Morgan that he didn't believe it possible for him to have the gift of music as he knew him to have the voice of a crow and fingers like thumbs. So saying, he put his fingers in his ears and challenged Morgan to play the harp.

As soon as Morgan touched the strings, a burst of lively music sprang from the harp and Evan Jones couldn't stop himself from dancing. Being neither an agile nor a fit man, he didn't normally dance, and when he danced he didn't dance normally. In a matter of minutes he was breathless and his sides began to ache. After a few more minutes he felt pains in his chest and down his arm as he begged for the music to stop. Morgan, realising this was the chance to teach him a lesson for all the upset he had caused over the years, just played on. Clutching his chest, Evan Jones dropped to the floor, causing Morgan to remove his fingers from the harp and so allowing the music to stop. Morgan helped Evan Jones to his feet and led him out of the door, up the slope and through the door to his cottage. Once Morgan had settled Evan Jones into his chair, he headed back down the slope. As he opened the door to his cottage he heard voices in the wind and looked round to hear the words, 'Fairy gifts should never be used in spite.' But no one was to be seen. Entering the living room, he looked to the corner of the room to discover that the golden harp had disappeared back to where it had come from.

However, things looked up as soon as Anna returned home. Morgan told her of all that had happened, just as I have told you. When she heard 'Jones the Sneer' had got his comeuppance, she hooted with laughter. Morgan told Anna that he was sad that he had not had the chance to play beautiful music for her on the golden harp. She told him not to fret as she would always be there to play and sing for him and their home would always be a happy and musical place. Now all she had to do was heat up the bake stone to make a new batch of Welsh cakes to fill up the empty tin. Later that evening, as they enjoyed their tea and freshly made Welsh cakes, Morgan and Anna reflected on the lesson that Morgan had learnt from the fairies and wondered if Evan Jones was also reflecting on the lesson he had been taught that day.

from
orchard
and
hedgerow

Part II

FROM ORCHARD & HEDGEROW

An apple, a pear, a peach or a cherry
Any good thing to make us merry

Blackberry Ginny

*In 1991, when I was North Pennines Storyteller-in-residence,
he hosted a community storytelling evening in the County
Durham village of Howden-le-Wear, where a lady who never
gave her name told me the story that follows. As a child she had
grown up in the small pit village of Easington, where there
lived a strange old woman who always seemed to be out picking
blackberries from the hedgerow. The children all thought her a
witch and would sometimes catcall after her 'Blackberry Ginny!
Blackberry Ginny!' That memory led her to tell me this story.*

Union miners stand together.
Do not heed the owner's tale,
Keep your hand upon your wages
And keep your eyes upon the scale.

So sang the miners of Easington colliery when they were
striking many years ago. The days turned into weeks and
the weeks to months as the strike held. Without wages,
the men still had wives and children to feed. The pitmen
were forced to become hunter-gatherers. One morning, the

miners gathered on the Easington foreshore. This was the spot where a dirty grey and coal dust beach touched the North Sea, for Easington was one of those pits where the coal seams the miners worked stretched for several miles under the seabed.

Standing on the shore before the men stood a fine jack hare. The men realised that if they could only catch the hare they could make a stew that would feed their families for a week. One man tried to dive on the animal to catch it, but with a flash of its white fur the hare spun on the spot before speeding off inland to the east. Ripping off their jackets, the miners chased after the hare. As you know, hares are very fast and can run great distances before they tire. Ahead the pitmen could see a thick hedge ten feet tall, perhaps, just perhaps? Without breaking its stride, the white hare cleared the hedge with a foot to spare. The best the miners could do was to run to the nearest gate and peer over. There was no sign of the hare, but on the other side of the hedge was Blackberry Ginny picking blackberries from the hedgerow – and it was March!

The pitmen knew if they were to catch that hare they would need the help of a fast dog. One of the miners had a brother who worked at Durham Jail, where they kept a bloodhound for the purpose of catching escaped prisoners. Surely that could help. The following day they borrowed this hound and again gathered on the beach. Sure enough, there stood the white hare looking invincible. The dog was loosed and once again the hare spun on the spot, racing inland to the east, pursued by the bloodhound. The dog chased the hare and the miners chased the dog. As this chase approached the thick, high hedge the miners watched, expecting the hare to jump, but it didn't. It spun on the spot, turning back towards Easington village, the small cluster of terraced pitman cottages where Blackberry Ginny lived in a terraced end house. The hare, the hound and the men turned down the back lane between the two rows of terraced houses. Approaching the high wooden gate that marked the entrance to Blackberry Ginny's small back yard, the dog sprang, its teeth nipping one of the strong back legs of the hare. Tiny drops of blood could be seen on the white fur. Still the hare had the strength and determination to leap over the high gate. The miners pushed open the wooden-slatted gate to reveal blood on the cobbles of the tiny yard. There was no sign of the hare! The miners rushed straight to the back door and with a greeting shout, pushed it open. Looking around, they still saw no sign of the hare, but Blackberry Ginny was sitting in a big wooden chair in the corner of the room … and she was bandaging her ankle! Knowing the striking miners and their families were hungry, Ginny gave several jars of her blackberry jelly to the men to share between them.

They never saw the hare on the shoreline ever again.

Dividing Apples

As boys, our hobby was scrumping apples. Although this was technically theft, we didn't class it as that. If you were caught, the worst punishment was just a clip around the ear, unless you'd taken some of the farmer's cider apples! While cider apples make a very fine drink, a lot of them taste horrible as 'eaters', so they would possibly be used as missiles. The farmer rightly considered this a waste of good fruit, making it probable that he'd have less cider to drink that year. This meant the offenders might even attract the attention of the local 'bobby', the strong arm of the law!

Two lads from the village of Merriott in Somerset had enjoyed a profitable day scrumping apples. They each had an armful and were looking for somewhere discreet to divide their ill-gotten gains. As it was just turning dark, they decided the safest place would be the churchyard. As they went through the big iron gates, one of them dropped two bright red apples by the gate. These apples are to become significant later in our tale.

Looking for somewhere to share out their spoils, they spotted a freshly dug grave. Great, if they climbed into the empty grave no one would ever spot them. Climbing in, they squatted to start their calculations. 'One for me … one for thee, two for me … two for thee…' Now it just happened that some petty theft had been going on in that area; in fact, the silver candlesticks had been stolen from Hinton St George church only the week before. This meant that the Merriott village 'bobby' was on his rounds. He cycled up the hill to the church, parked his bike against the iron railings and shone his torch around the churchyard. The beam of light passed over the top of the open grave and he saw nothing. Suspicious beyond reason, he cocked up his ears and heard, 'One for me … one for thee … two for me … two for thee …' Leaping back on his bike, he tore back down the hill to the local police station – they move pretty fast down in the West Country! Racing up to the counter, he told the sergeant that they had a problem as he'd heard God and the Devil in the churchyard dividing up the souls of all the folk in the village. The sergeant, who was as round as he was tall, decided they should go back together to investigate. Climbing on to their 'sit up and beg' bicycles, they wobbled up the hill. By the time they'd struggled to the top their faces were bright red.

Leaning their bikes against the iron gates, where the two red apples had been dropped, they shone their torches over the tops of the gravestones. The twin beams of light passed over the open grave where the two lads were dividing the apples. The two policemen pricked up their ears and listened. 'One for me … one for thee … two for me … two for thee … and that's all …' Then one of the lads chirped up, 'That's all … what about those two bright red ones we left by the gate?'

Well the two policemen screamed in terror, jumped on their bikes and tore off down the road. They were still screaming and thinking they were being chased by 'Old Nick' when they cycled through the next village half an hour later.

The boys took the apples home and their families enjoyed a fine supper of baked apples that night.

Just Desserts

The following is a little-known English folk tale, which I have reworked and retitled for this collection. The motif of soft fruit magically growing out of season is common in Eastern Europe, where the climate can be much colder and inclement. It was great to find such a tale from this small island, where we are now trying to live and eat with the seasons. The pantheist nature of the tale chimes with me, especially as two of my favourite tales in my repertoire are 'The Wonderful Wood' and 'The Vixen and the Oakmen', both from Somerset folklorist Ruth Tongue, one of my mentors. Although 'Just Desserts' is not from this source, I feel it is cut from the same cloth. One of my mentees once gifted me the following riddle:

> My skin is red, pale within
> Golden specks upon my skin
> Sometimes sour, sometimes sweet
> You will find me growing at your feet
> What am I?
> The answer is in this tale …

Many years ago, next to a large wood there were two houses. The biggest of these was the home of a farmer, an ill-mannered and mean man. He was so mean he seemed to begrudge sharing the very air we breathe. He was the sort of man who, if he was pouring you a drink and you said stop, he did!

Next door was a tumbledown cottage, the home of an old couple who were so poor they thought knives and forks were jewellery. Because folk in the village knew this old pair were as poor as church mice they brought them their leftovers, or the odd spare vegetable or bone to make a nourishing soup. When these gifts arrived the old man and woman made it their business to smile and say the grateful words 'Thank you'.

This always so pleased and delighted their visitors from the village that they would return the following week with more gifts just to see their grateful smiles and hear their grateful words of thanks. The farmer next door was so mean-spirited that he would rather have thrown his leftover food away than share it with his neighbours.

The old couple didn't even have a strip of land on which to grow their own food; all they had was a border the size of a doormat outside their front door. Every day their nanny goat could be seen standing on this piece of dirt. If the goat leaned too far towards the hedge that divided their humble dwelling from the farmer's land he would come out and bash the hedge with a stick to scare the goat, saying that it was stealing the leaves from his hedge and casting a shadow over his rose bushes.

One day, terrified, the goat ran over the road and into the nearby wood. This meant big trouble. The grumpy farmer, who claimed he owned the wood, might fancy a goat stew for supper and it would mean no more milk. The old couple, however, had grown up knowing that it was an oak wood and as 'fairy folk live in old oaks', never mind the farmer, it was more important to ask permission of the oak men to enter the wood. Chasing after the goat, the old couple whispered, 'Please may we enter your wood,' to the oldest and wisest grandfather oak. From the great trunk of the tree tiny voices answered that the old couple were welcome, thus ensuring their safe passage into the wood to retrieve their goat and out again when they were ready to leave. The old couple smiled, whispered their thank you to the oak men and, entering the wood, caught up with the goat.

Looking down, the old man and woman were surprised to see their goat wasn't eating grass, but was eating ripe and juicy wild strawberries growing at their feet. The old couple hadn't eaten a strawberry for a long time, but seeing so many, asked the oak men if it would be alright just to try one. They were told that was fine and they could take some home with them. They once again gave their thanks to the little men and, taking a small runner of strawberries, made their way out of the wood, with the goat, back to the cottage. They placed the runners on their tiny border by their front door, where they instantly rooted and grew. By the evening that plant was heavy with ripe strawberries, and also when they milked the goat the milk was richer and creamier than it had ever been.

Looking over the hedge, the farmer noticed the strawberry plant and asked where it had come from. When they told him it was from the wood, he became furious. As it was his wood they must be his strawberries. He couldn't bear anyone to have something he didn't. Without a 'please' or a 'thank you', the farmer stormed round and started to gorge himself on the strawberries. The old couple didn't try to stop him, as they had seen that the strawberries had magically grown immediately and even when picked, more seemed to keep growing.

Sure enough, the following morning the strawberry plant had plenty for the old couple.

Jealous, the old farmer set out to seek the magical strawberry plants in the wood.

Without even acknowledging the existence of the oak men, or indeed asking any permission to enter, he stormed into the wood. In doing this he was to ensure that he would never again come out. Finding the wild strawberries, he started to gorge upon them like a man possessed. He simply could not stop eating. Pick and gorge, pick and gorge. If he hadn't burst he'd still be there eating!

As for the old couple who well knew the value of the magic words 'please' and 'thank you', the folk of the village continued to care for them. They also always seemed to have strawberries and creamy goat's milk whatever the season.

Sweet and Sour Berries

We storytellers collect our stories from every source. At a conference I once heard Jack Zipes describe us as 'honest thieves'. I have taken the bones of the story that follows from Chinese-American storyteller Linda Fang. We have yet to meet but have both contributed stories to More Ready-to-Tell Tales from Around the World, *compiled by David Holt and Bill Mooney, two wonderful American tellers. This book is full of folk tales for all to share and tell. Recently foraging for food has increased in popularity as we have rediscovered the bounty provided by nature to rich and poor alike. Even top chefs now use foragers as part of their teams.*

Jack lived in a tiny cottage with his mother and they were mortal poor. All that they could afford every month was a sack of flour that Jack's mother turned into loaves of bread, while Jack went out with a basket foraging for free food. Jack would find mushrooms, wild herbs, berries and bird eggs to turn into a simple meal.

One sad day Jack returned with a good basket of field mushrooms, wild garlic and Easter ledge to discover the back door of the cottage smashed. While he had been away, burglars had been in and robbed his mother. He found her tied to a chair, shaken but thankfully unharmed. She told him that they had taken the one remaining bag of flour and all of their loaves of bread. What were they to do? As it was autumn, Jack told his mother that he would return to the wood and collect a basket of wild berries, her favourite, for their supper and to make her feel a bit better.

He walked mile after mile before he found a bush full of sweet, black berries. As he was picking them into his basket he made up a little song:

> One for Mother, one for me
> One for Mother, one for me

As he sang, Jack didn't notice that behind a nearby bush was one of the burglars watching him.

Jack took the berries home and his mother adored them. As she ate one after another she no longer felt hungry. She was so pleased that Jack told her the next morning he would return to the same bush for more. As good as his word, he was up at the crack of dawn and off to the woods with two baskets. When he reached the bush, he burst into tears; someone had got there before him, not even leaving enough berries to fill one basket. Jack was forced to walk miles farther before he found two more berry bushes standing side by side. He tasted a berry from the nearest bush. It was sweet – that was good. Then he tasted a berry from the other bush. It was sour, not so good. He started to pick the berries from both bushes, separating them into two baskets while singing:

> Sweet for Mother, sour for me
> Sweet for Mother, sour for me

Jack was then shocked to find that standing next to him was a stranger. He realised that it must be one of the burglars. The stranger asked Jack what he was singing, so again he sang:

> Sweet for Mother, sour for me,
> Sweet for Mother, sour for me

Jack was amazed to notice a tear appear in the stranger's eye and trickle down his cheek. He asked why a grown man was crying. The burglar told Jack that he hadn't seen his own mother for many months since he had left home to join the gang of thieves. As Jack, however, was caring for his mother then he would leave them in peace to manage the best they could. With this the two smiled and went their separate ways. Jack picked up his baskets and slowly headed home to his mother and the burglar to who knows where.

By the time Jack got back to greet his mother at their cottage door there was a sack of flour on the doorstep with a note that read, 'I hope this flour will help you through the hard times – from your friend in the wood.' Jack's mother set to and baked bread before the two of them sat down to share the sweet berries, because they shared everything.

The Pear Pip

I was gifted this story many years ago by storyteller friends Rick Wilson and Helen East. A version of my telling of the tale featured on Undefeated, an audio in support of miners. I love it and have passed it on to many others.

When the sun was strong and the weather hot, the young farm labourer would venture into the orchard and rest in the shade of the pear tree, and couldn't he help himself to a pear! This was a delight to an overworked and poorly paid young man. Sometimes he would fall asleep in the shade of the tree and just dream. On one such day he had fallen asleep, exhausted from having been out at the dead of night to steal a loaf of bread. Just one loaf of bread to feed his starving wife and children! Word of this had got out and the constables arrived to arrest him while he was there dozing, and he was too slow to put up a fight. He was marched off to the nearby castle dungeon.

Now it just happened that in his jacket pocket was a small pear that he was keeping for later. So this poor man was arrested and thrown in to prison for stealing just one loaf of bread to keep body and soul together. As he slumped on to the straw-covered stone floor and looked up to the iron bars of the window he nibbled the pear from his pocket and he had an idea … a cunning plan.

The young man told his jailer, a brute of a man, that he wished to see the king. The jailer asked what the scum of the earth such as him could possibly want with the king.

The young man told the jailer that he had a gift for the king. This message was conveyed to the king, whose curiosity was aroused. He ordered that the prisoner be brought to him. Shackles were hammered around the prisoner's ankle and he was dragged up the stone steps of the castle with the chains rattling step after step. Sitting on his splendid throne, the king looked down upon the sorry sight of the prisoner. He asked the young man what gift he could ever have that was fit for a king. The young man put his hand in his jacket pocket and took out a single pear pip. Showing this to the king, he told him that it was a magic pear pip that, if planted by an honest man, would grow a tree that would bear golden fruit. The young man pointed out that he was not able to plant it for he was not an honest man, having stolen one loaf of bread; but perhaps His Majesty the King could. He reminded the king that if it was planted by an honest man it would grow a tree that would bear golden fruit. The king looked at the seed and was just about to take it, and then he remembered a day when he was very young on which his mother the old queen wasn't looking, he had taken a gold coin from her purse just to have money of his own. He realised that he may not be honest enough to plant the seed. He told the young prisoner to hand the seed to the jailer.

The jailer was reminded that if the pear pip was planted by an honest man it would grow a tree that would bear golden fruit. The jailer was just about to take the seed when he remembered a time that he had taken a bribe from a prisoner to allow a visit from his wife to his cell and so was not honest enough to plant the seed.

The lord chamberlain, who had been observing the proceedings and seeing the hesitation of the jailer, stepped forward and the young man quickly offered him the pear pip, bowing and saying that if it was planted by an honest man it would grow a tree that would bear golden fruit. The chamberlain was just about to take the pear pip when he thought about the time that he had been in competition for his role as chancellor and had falsely accused his opponent in order to secure his position. He stepped back, realising that he was not honest enough to plant the seed.

The king sent for his chief judge, the very person who would stand in judgement over the young man. This guardian of law and order arrived and the young prisoner, still with the pear pip in his hand, offered it to the judge, telling him that if it was planted by an honest man it would grow a tree that would bear golden fruit. The judge was just about to take the seed when he remembered the time that in the dock before him stood a man he knew to be guilty but because he was a family friend he allowed him to walk free. He knew he was not honest enough to take the seed.

The prisoner turned to the king and remarked that there with him were three rich, important or supposedly law-abiding people yet not one of them was honest enough to plant a simple pear pip. He, however, was imprisoned for stealing just one loaf of bread to feed his starving family. On hearing this, the king thought deeply, nodded and ordered the jailer to release the shackles and let the young prisoner free.

As the young man set off for home walking away from the castle, he took from his pocket a simple pear pip, smiled, flicked the pip into the hedge and skipped off down the road towards home and the pear tree in the orchard that had saved his life. Passing the pear tree, he filled his pockets with some of the fruit and made his way to his cottage. There he was surrounded by his family, who were of course delighted by his safe return. That evening, as they sat down to enjoy a supper of poached pears, the young man told them the story of how a simple pear pip had helped to secure his freedom. And that is the story I have just told to you.

The Yazzle Tree

I have fond memories of searching out and picking fresh hazelnuts with my dad when I was a lad, so I wanted this story included. Nuts are part of the bounty of the hedgerow and a healthy addition to our diet.

The story that follows is an exception in this collection in that it is not from the tongue of Taffy Thomas. Although I have lived for more than forty years in Lakeland, I have never felt it fit to impersonate the rich and increasingly rare dialects of Cumberland and Westmorland, but I do love to hear their rich tones. The tale is from the tongue of my friend, Edward Acland, who grew up hearing it from his grandfather. Edward still lives and works from Sprint Mill, one of the oldest mills in Cumbria, where he and his wife Romola continue to be an inspiration with their environmental projects. The tale also embraces the Lakeland tradition of tall tales in the county that hosts the Biggest Liar in the World competition.

Thanks Edward and your forbears.

Ah was doon ut suthen end of't Bassenthut leeak a ponderin ower how ah was garn tu git yam in time fur mi bait. As misses-body, quite reetly so, was reet particular a beeat punctuality at meal times. Ah'd two miles to ga to git yam in er cuppler minits if ah wus gunner be on time for mi bait.

Anyroad, as ah was ponderin ower mi dilemma ah sees this gut fish cumin oop'd beck, an been a quick thinkin lad, as t'fish gars oonder't brig ah givs a gut lowp an lands reet in't middul of t'fishes back, which, as yer can imagin, was a lile bit slee-ap, an ah wus wurrid a beeat tummelin off intut water … so ah rammed mi yazzel stick reet doon intut fishes back an ah held on tu't yazzel stick fur grim death.

An we gars oop Bassenthut lee-ak wi a gut wee-av on yan side an a gut wee-av on t'other, joost like yanna them/there Trident sumpherines. An wen wi gits tut t'other end of t' thwait ah givs er gut lowp an lands on't tut brig at t'other end of t'leeak … an yan minit laiter ah'm yam, reet on tyme fur mi bait … misses-body reet chuffed, an gave us er lile cuddle. 'Ah can orlus rely on yu milad,' shi ses. Ah niver let on 'ow ah'd gitten there on tyme.

Anyroad, this isn't t'end of tut tale … fur abeeat a year later ah wus doon at suthen end of tut thwaite agin, beeat seeam brig wen ah sees seeam fish cumin' oop'd beeak. Ah cud tell it was seeam fish, for, dammit, mi yazzel stick had teken root in't tut fishes back, an as t'fish gars oonder't brig ah leeans ower an ah gather three punds of fresh yazzel nuts off its branches.

My friend Edward Acland has contributed this translation to the story to help the linguistically challenged unfamiliar with the rich poetic dialect of Lakeland.

I was down at the southern end of Bassenthwaite Lake pondering over how I was going to get home in time for my tea, as my wife, quite rightly so, was very particular about punctuality at meal times. I had two miles to go to get home in a couple of minutes if I was going to be on time for my tea.

Anyway, as I was pondering over my dilemma, I noticed a large fish coming up the beck, and being a quick-thinking lad, as the fish went under the bridge, I did a great leap and landed right in the middle of the fish's back, which as you can imagine, was a bit slippery, and I was worried about tumbling off into the cold water – so I rammed my hazel stick right down into the fish's back, and I held on for grim death.

And we went up Bassenthwaite Lake with a huge wave on one side and a huge wave on the other, just like one of those Trident submarines. And when we got to the other end of the 'thwaite I did a great leap again and landed on the bridge at the other end of the lake – and one minute later I was home, right on time for my tea. My wife was very pleased with me and gave me a little cuddle. 'I can always rely on you my lad,' she says. I never did let her know how I'd got there on time!

Anyway, this isn't the end of the tale. For about a year later, I was down at the southern end of the 'thwaite again, by the same bridge, when I saw the same fish coming up the beck. I could tell it was the same fish, for damn it, my hazel stick had taken root in the fish's back, and as the fish went under the bridge, I leaned over and gathered three pounds of best fresh hazelnuts off its branches.

Part III

THE STORYTELLER'S SUPPER

MENU

for a Storyteller's Supper

starter
KITCHEN GARDEN SALAD
WITH THE QUEEN BEE'S HONEY DRESSING
SERVED WITH
THE PARSLEY QUEEN'S HERB SCONES

soup
TURNIP & SAGE SOUP FIT FOR A KING

entree
GIANT'S POTTED SHRIMPS
FOLLOWED BY
CHESHIRE CHEESE & ONION PIE

dessert
POOR MAN'S POACHED PEARS
SERVED WITH
BLACKBERRY GINNY'S BRAMBLE JELLY
AND FOLLOWED BY
FAIRY CAKES

You can try out this menu and share the food and the stories,
or create a menu of your own with different stories from the book
and your favourite recipes alongside.

Kitchen Garden Salad with the Queen Bee's Honey Dressing

See The Queen Bee in FROM THE KITCHEN GARDEN

Ingredients

8 cherry tomatoes
1 lettuce
1 cucumber
1 carrot
A few radishes
1 tbsp clear honey
1 tbsp balsamic vinegar
2 tbsp extra virgin olive oil
A pinch of sea salt

Method

1. Wash and cut the cherry tomatoes into halves. Clean and wash the lettuce. Wash and slice the cucumber. Wash, peel and grate the carrot. Wash and slice the radishes.

2. Mix the honey and balsamic vinegar in a bowl. Add olive oil and sea salt to taste.

3. Assemble lettuce leaves in a salad bowl with the cherry tomatoes and cucumber slices. Pour over the salad dressing and then decorate the salad with the grated carrot and sliced radishes.

The Parsley Queen's Herb Scones

See 'The Parsley Queen' in FROM THE KITCHEN GARDEN

Ingredients

250g (8oz) self-raising flour, white or wholemeal
50g (2oz) butter
150ml (¼ pint) buttermilk or fresh milk
2 tbsp chopped fresh parsley or mixed herbs
Extra milk to glaze

Method

1. Sieve flour into mixing bowl and cut butter into small pieces. Rub the butter lightly into the flour.

2. Stir fresh herbs into the rubbed-in mixture.

3. Make a well in the centre of the mixture and pour in buttermilk. Mix to a soft dough and turn out on to a floured board.

4. Knead dough until smooth then roll or pat out until about 18mm (¾in) thick.

5. Cut into rounds with fluted cutter or with a sharp knife cut into triangles.

6. Place on a lightly greased baking tray and glaze with milk.

7. Bake at 230C (gas mark 8) for 8–10 minutes until risen and golden brown. A little grated cheese can also be added to the glaze.

Turnip & Sage Soup
fit for a King

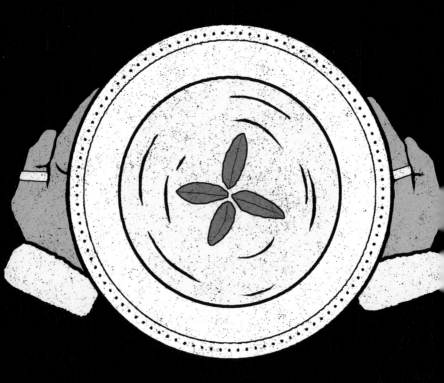

See 'The Princess of Turnips'
in FROM THE KITCHEN GARDEN

Ingredients

50g (2oz) butter
1 medium onion, chopped
450g (1lb) turnips, chopped
1 large potato, chopped
1 litre (2 pints) vegetable stock
Salt and freshly milled black pepper
6 fresh sage leaves
6 tbsp cream, natural yoghurt or buttermilk
6 purple sage leaves, to garnish

Method

1. Melt butter in a large saucepan and add the onion. Cover with a lid and cook until the onion is soft, but not coloured.

2. Add the turnips and potato, stir and continue to cook gently for 10 minutes.

3. Pour in the stock, cover and simmer gently for about 20 minutes until the vegetables are soft.

4. Season with salt and pepper, then liquidise with the fresh sage leaves.

5. Return to a clean pan and reheat gently.

6. Serve with swirls of cream, yoghurt or buttermilk and garnish with purple sage leaves.

Giant's Potted Shrimps

See 'Shrimps for a Giant' in FROM SEA AND SHORE

Ingredients

125g unsalted butter (plus 50g extra)
Grating of fresh nutmeg
Pinch of ground cinnamon
Pinch of cayenne pepper
400g peeled brown shrimp
Brown bread & butter and lemon wedges to serve

Method

1. Melt the butter in a pan and add the spices with a pinch of sea salt.

2. Add shrimp and coat well.

3. Divide among 6 small ramekins, then chill in fridge until set.

4. Melt the 50g butter in a pan and strain off the clear butter at the top (discard the solid bits).

5. Pour the clarified butter over the shrimps and chill for at least 2 hours. Then serve with the brown bread and butter and lemon wedges. (The clarified butter acts as a seal and can be discarded if preferred.)

Cheshire
Cheese

&

Onion
Pie

See 'The Cheshire Cheese that went to Heaven'
in FROM FARMYARD AND DAIRY

Ingredients

275g plain flour
180g salted butter (140g cut into cubes)
2–3 tbsp cold water
3 onions (sliced)
3 banana shallots
1 tbsp thyme leaves (chopped)
400g Cheshire cheese (grated)
1 free-range egg (beaten)

Method

1. Sift flour into a bowl. Add the cubed butter and rub in until the mixture resembles coarse breadcrumbs.
2. Add cold water and using a knife draw the pastry together. Wrap in clingfilm and chill for 30 minutes. (You can use ready-made short crust pastry if preferred.)
3. Meanwhile, add the remaining butter to pan with the onions, shallots and thyme. Cook gently for 15 minutes, without colouring. Add 180ml water and cook until evaporated and the onions are cooked.
4. Preheat oven to 180C (gas 4).
5. Roll out half of the pastry to about 0.5cm thick and line a 25cm pie dish. Roll out the other pastry to make lid.
6. Cover the base of the pie with half the cooked onion, mixture followed by half the cheese and repeat again, seasoning with white pepper between the layers.
7. Brush the edge with beaten egg and lay the lid on top. Seal the pie by crimping.
8. Brush the pie with the rest of the egg and cut a slit in the top for steam to escape.
9. Place the pie on to a heated baking sheet and bake for 40–45 minutes until golden brown.

Poor Man's Poached Pears

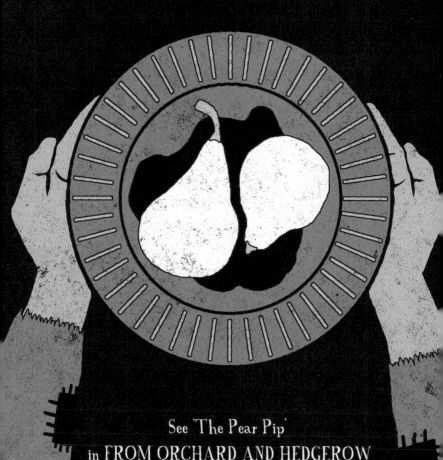

See 'The Pear Pip'
in FROM ORCHARD AND HEDGEROW

Ingredients

300g sugar
2½ tbsp lemon juice
½ cinnamon stick
4 cloves
1 vanilla bean
4 pears

Method

1. Use a saucepan large enough to hold 4 upright pears, plus their stalks. Put the sugar and 750ml water into the pan over a low heat and stir until the sugar has dissolved. Now bring to the boil and add lemon juice, cinnamon stick, cloves and vanilla bean.

2. Peel the pears, keeping the stalks attached. Place upright in the pan, cover and poach gently for 30–45 minutes, or until tender. Remove pears to serving bowls and simmer the syrup until it thickens slightly.

3. Spoon a little syrup over the pears. Serve warm or chilled with cream or ice cream.

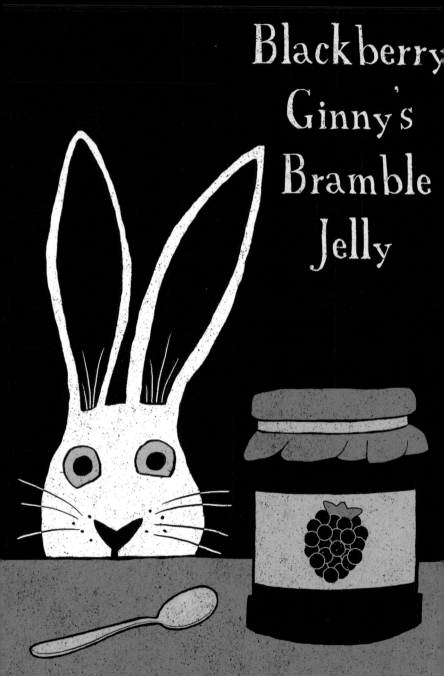

Blackberry
Ginny's
Bramble
Jelly

See 'Blackberry Ginny' in FROM ORCHARD AND HEDGEROW

Ingredients

2lb blackberries
150ml (¼ pint) cold water
4 tbsp lemon juice
400g (14oz) sugar to each 600ml (1 pint) juice

Method

1. Put blackberries in a pan with the water and simmer very gently for 25–30 minutes until soft. Strain through a muslin-lined sieve or a jelly bag for at least a couple of hours or overnight.

2. Measure the strained juice and put in a large pan with the lemon juice. Add the appropriate amount of sugar and heat gently, stirring until the sugar is dissolved.

3. Bring to the boil and boil rapidly until setting point is reached.

4. Pour into warmed, sterilised jars and seal tightly. Enjoy with hot, buttered toast, scones or even with poached pears!

Fairy Cakes

See 'A Baker for the Fairies' in FROM FIELD AND FURROW

Ingredients

125g salted butter
125g caster sugar
2 eggs
125g (4oz) self-raising flour
5ml (1 tsp) vanilla extract
15ml (1tbsp) milk

For the buttercream icing
150g unsalted butter
250g icing sugar
10ml (2 tsp) vanilla extract
60ml (4 tbsp) strawberry jam
Icing sugar, for dusting

Method

1. Preheat oven to 180C (gas 4). Line a muffin tin with paper cases.
2. Put butter and sugar into a bowl and whisk until light and fluffy. Gradually beat in the eggs.
3. Sift the flour into the mixture and gently fold in until well combined. Stir in the vanilla essence and milk.
4. Spoon the mixture into the paper cases and cook for 18–20 minutes.
5. For the icing, put the butter in a bowl and beat until creamy. Sift in the icing sugar and whisk until combined. Add vanilla extract and a little milk if the mixture is too stiff.
6. Cut the top off each cake and then cut the slices in half. Cover each cake with the butter icing. Put a little jam on top of each cake and then push the 2 half-slices into the icing at an angle, to make a pair of wings.
7. Dust with icing sugar and serve.

from
farmyard
and
dairy

Part IV

FROM FARMYARD AND DAIRY

Sun is coming up, farmer's out the door.
He will go to milk the cow, and start his daily chores.
Sun is going down, horse is in the stable.
All the fields are planted now, supper's on the table.

The Milkmaid and Her Pail

*As a boy in the 1950s holidaying on my maternal grandparents'
small farm in Somerset I enjoyed following my grandfather and
his labourer, Cecil, into the cowshed for milking. The task was
accomplished by hand as we had no machine in those days. They
would sit on three-legged stools with their foreheads pressed against
the sides of the black-and-white Friesian cows as they squeezed
their pink teats and foaming milk squirted into steel pails, making
an almost machine gun rattle. When the pails were full they would
be carried back to the dairy suspended on a yoke, a length of wood
carved to fit across the shoulders and behind the neck of the carrier.
The pails were attached to each end by a short chain and hook. With
a yoke it was possible to transport two buckets at once. We never
had a milkmaid unless you counted my aunt, always a tomboy, who
loved to come and help. The milkmaid in this tale was working
before yokes were in use and could only carry one pail at a time; as
was the way in peasant culture, she carried it on her head.*

In far-off Greece there was a milkmaid who was dreamer.
As she went about her work she eased the day's labours by

musing. One dreamy day, while carrying a foaming pail of milk on her head, she mused that the sale of that milk might make sufficient money to buy three hundred eggs. With luck those eggs could produce two hundred and fifty chicks. If those chicks were nurtured they would become chickens that could be sold to a butcher when the price was right. Wouldn't she rightfully get a share of the profits?

She decided in her head that she would use her share of the money to buy a beautiful gown to wear to the village dance. Wouldn't she look so beautiful in that dress that all the handsome young men would crowd around her and ask for a dance? If she didn't like their attention then she would toss her head and send them on their way.

By now she was so immersed in this dream that as she imagined haughtily tossing her head she actually did toss her head, and yes you've guessed it, her pail tumbled to the ground and all of the milk drained into the dirt, together with her dreams.

> A maiden a-milking did go
> A maiden a-milking did go
> And the wind it did blow high
> And the wind it did blow low
> And it blew her pail to and fro
> > Traditional

The Cheshire Cheese that Went to Heaven

As a teenager in the 1960s I was taken to a tiny Somerset cottage to meet Ruth Tongue, the elderly eccentric folklorist and storyteller. She told me a number of tales, we drank copious quantities of

*strong tea and she hugely encouraged and inspired me. The tale
that follows is my version of one she collected from her uncle, who
heard it in Cheshire in the 1860s.*

*The chorus from the song I use to precede the tale was the
creation of another remarkable eccentric, Leslie Howarth, a
Cheshire fruit farmer.*

> Here's to Cheshire, here's to cheese,
> Here's to the pears and the apple trees,
> Here's to the lovely strawberries …

Many years ago in Cheshire there lived a farmer's wife
whose pride and joy was her creamery. The fame of her
butter and cheese spread throughout the county. Because
of this, she got a weekly visit from the local priest, who
came ostensibly to bring her a scripture, although in truth
the regularity of his visits was fed by the knowledge that
she kept a good kitchen. The woman feared his visits would
eat her out of house and home.

As she made the best cheese in the whole of Cheshire, she
thought she might outface the greedy priest and keep him at
bay by making a truckle of cheese for him as big as a wagon
wheel. When the ever-hungry priest arrived on the following
week he couldn't resist peeking into the creamery. The giant
round cheese was a sight to behold. As the priest licked his
chops, the woman told him that the cheese was not quite
ready for eating yet. She assured him, however, that as soon
as it was ready it would be transported to his presbytery on a
hay wagon as a gift. Although the clergyman smiled at this
prospect, as soon as the woman's back was turned he couldn't
resist stretching out his podgy fingers and pinching a largish
chunk of the creamy cheese. The cheese, strangely, was aware

of its worth and role in life. Not liking being poked at and nibbled, it thought, 'I am for the needy, not for the greedy.'

It rolled off the table and out of the creamery door. Rolling past the barn entrance, and with a lump already missing, things got worse. The two sheepdogs that were kept in the barn ran out on their long rope tether and managed to snaffle a couple of mouthfuls from the cheese. With a large piece of its original perfect circle gone, the cheese muttered again, 'I am for the needy, not for the greedy,' and, rolling down the hill, escaped the barking dogs.

Halfway down the hill, who should the cheese encounter but Old Daddy Fox. Clasped in his jaws was a plump duck. A large chunk of creamy cheese struck Reynard as a more attractive proposition, so he dropped the duck at the roadside before helping himself to three good bites of the cheese. Just then the fox heard the sound it most feared, namely the sound of a horn and the yapping of hounds. The fox fled, even forgetting to pick up the dead duck. He was full of cheese but his vixen and cubs would go hungry that night.

Now much smaller than its original size, the cheese thought that perhaps it could still make a goodish meal for someone who was 'needy, not greedy'. Ahead the cheese could see a flock of geese. Rolling through the middle of that gaggle would probably see the end of every last crumb of the cheese, so it swerved past the birds and up a lane to the side.

There, sitting on a grassy bank, who should the cheese come across but three blind starving beggars. At last, the cheese thought, I've found the 'needy, not the greedy', if only there were more of me left for them. However, for three men who wouldn't have eaten for many days, the remainder of the cheese split three ways equally was more than enough, and only one crumb got left.

Accompanied by a flash of light, the three beggars stood up and revealed that they had wings. Indeed they were angels, and guess what … the cheese was made whole again and, sprouting wings, found itself floating towards heaven alongside the other three: a reward for the generosity and kind nature it had shown.

So … 'Here's to Cheshire, Here's to cheese …'

Salt in the Milk

Salt has long played a part in the preservation of food through the seasons as part of a salting and pickling process, especially in the years before the invention of the freezer, when there was a surfeit of produce – better than waste.

In times past it was believed that salt left at the entrance to a house would protect the inhabitants from visits by fairies, sprites or spirits. Farmers would leave a pile of salt next to the churn of milk on their doorstep. In this story the farmer remembers to put out the churn but forgets the pile of salt!

With salt having this history and mystery it is not surprising that it features in a number of folk tales, making it a must at the Storyteller's Supper. The tale that follows I fondly remember sharing with a Westmorland farmer and his family at the foot of the famous Fairy Steps in Beetham while the family enjoyed their picnic. I had been invited to tell local stories as the guest of the Area of Natural Beauty group. Their picnic just happened to include hard-boiled eggs and a pinch of salt! Please tell the tale at your next picnic or just take it with a pinch of salt!

On the northern shore of Morecambe Bay there was once a farmer who had a farm about the size of a pocket handkerchief. His land was just big enough for his tiny cottage, one meadow and one cow. Every evening he milked the cow and stood the little cast iron milk churn on the doorstep of his cottage. This would keep the milk nice and cool. At the same time he would always put a little pile of salt next to the churn. The salt was there to act as protection against a visit from fairies, sprites or spirits. One particular evening, when putting the churn on the doorstep, he clean forgot to place the pile of salt by it. The next morning, when he lifted the lid of the churn, the level of the milk inside was lower; someone or something must have stolen some of the milk.

Now the fairies living in the rocks on the bay shore had been blessed with a baby, so it was they who had taken a little milk to feed the fairy babe. The farmer, aggrieved, wanted to teach whoever had taken the milk a lesson. He went into the kitchen, where he noticed a small pile of salt still standing on the end of the dresser. Seeing the pile of salt, the farmer realised that by forgetting to put it on the doorstep he must have received a visit from the fairies. He grabbed a handful of salt, went back out to the step and tossed the salt into the milk churn. That would teach the culprits a lesson!

When the fairies returned that evening for milk to feed their baby, they tasted the milk, hated the taste of the salt, and spat it out over the farmer's land. Where they spat out the milk the grass died and nothing ever grew again.

As far as I know the fairy family are still happily living among the rocks on the shoreline. A neighbouring farmer who knew well the ways of the fairies and who, rather than leave a pile of salt, always left a tiny jug of milk for them, had become their next source of food for their baby. This farmer's land always seemed to prosper.

Perhaps the first farmer had learnt a lesson about being mean-spirited over such a small amount of milk …

The Chicken and the Egg

I was told this story by Bernard Tagliarini at one of the Society for Storytelling 'gatherings', events I am always proud to attend as a patron of the society. The story gets an annual outing just before the egg-rolling happens at Easter in the Storyteller's Garden in Grasmere.

The most stressed bird on this planet is the chicken. This fowl, a student of philosophy, wakes each morning wondering which came first, the chicken or the egg. Which do you think …?

One day a chicken decided to seek out the truth. It went to consult the wisest of birds, the owl of course. Heading towards the far side of the farmyard, she came to the old oak tree that boasted the nest of a tawny owl. The owl peered down from the nest to see the chicken at the foot of the tree. The owl enquired as to the reason for the chicken's visit and was told that the chicken wanted to pick the owl's brains as it had a perplexing question that was greatly troubling it. Which came first, the chicken or the egg? On hearing the question, the owl merely smiled and, reaching above its nest, took down an ancient dusty dictionary. Turning the pages – no mean feat with a wing and a clawed foot – the owl pronounced that chicken begins with a 'C' and egg with an 'E' so, going by the book, chicken should come first.

Just for a moment the chicken felt satisfied, but before it could completely relax the owl added that if, however, it considered itself not a chicken but a hen, then according to the book the egg came first. Now the chicken was thrown into confusion and stress. Was it a chicken or was it a hen? It was stressing about this so much it didn't notice a stirring in the hedge or see a flash of red fur as the two birds were joined by Old Daddy Fox. The greedy fox grabbed the chicken and gobbled it all up before it had even had the chance to forget about its philosophising and deal with the dilemma in order to save itself. So you see there are some things in life that it's not worth stressing about.

As for the farmer's wife, she collected the eggs for their tea as usual, but her chicken never returned that night and she never did find out what happened to it.

Chick, chick, chick, chick, chicken, lay a little egg for me
Chick, chick, chick, chick, chicken, I want one for my tea
I haven't had an egg since Easter and now it's half past three
So chick, chick, chick, chick, chicken, lay a little egg for me.

Oonagh's Special Soda Bread

In 1995, when I was the North Pennines Storyteller in Residence, I had the pleasure of the company of fellow storyteller Sally Greenaway when I visited her house to share tea, tales, and home-made buttered soda bread with jam. On one such visit she told me the story that follows. The message that the hero behind the story is the woman behind the man is the perfect metaphor for this author and his wife and muse. I particularly like that the story combines the naming of a famous Irish land feature with the mention of a famous Irish recipe.

It was said of the famous Irish hero Finn McCool that if his name wasn't mentioned every day the world would end, so we might have just saved the world! Finn, a giant of a man three metres tall and with hands the size of chair backs, lived with his wife Oonagh in a tiny cottage in the north of Ireland. Weren't they just the perfect married couple, for if Finn had the brawn, his wife Oonagh had the brains. Not only that, Oonagh was known to bake the finest soda bread on the Emerald Isle.

Finn had one enemy that he feuded with and this was a giant named Cuchulain. He was four metres tall with a long red beard and long red hair that he wore in a ponytail. Cuchulain was so quick he once caught a thunderbolt in his bare hands and pressed it into a pancake, which he kept in his waistcoat pocket to release when it was least expected. The other thing about Cuchulain was that all of his strength was in the middle finger of his left hand. This meant that if he clicked his fingers, it magically doubled his strength. If he clicked his fingers twice he had the strength of four giants. If he clicked them four times, the strength of eight giants and so on …

Finn had promised his wife Oonagh that he'd dig a well in the farmyard for her to fill the kettle to make the tea. Finn never got round to digging that well for he was the sort of man who liked the idea of 'do it yourself' but never got those jobs finished … Finn however wasn't lazy; he was just busy. He was building a causeway across the Irish Sea towards Scotland to facilitate his battles with the Scottish giants. This was a walkway of wood resting on hexagonal pillars of rock.

One day, as Finn was working on the causeway, he heard the skirl of the bagpipes. Peering to the east, who should he see in the distance but Cuchulain striding across the Irish Sea towards him with his long red beard and ponytail tossing in the breeze. Cuchulain had just returned from fighting the

Scottish giants, carrying the spoils of his battles. Indeed he was wearing a kilt and playing the bagpipes, the fiercest weapon to come out of Scotland! Cuchulain was so big and strong that he could wade across the sea with no need of a causeway and with his boots crushing the crabs on the seabed. Even though the tide was in, the water only came up to his belly button.

Finn just turned in shock and raced back up the hill towards the cottage and his loyal wife Oonagh. When she saw her husband racing up the hill with his face white as a ghost and his hair standing on end, she asked him why he was so feart. Finn told her that his fiercest enemy had come to fight him and would probably kill him with his magic middle finger. Oonagh told him not to be such a baby and that she would help him. Finn asked her how she could possibly help as she was only a woman! Oonagh told him that if he only did as she told him, things would all turn out to the good. She then told her husband that he must come into the cottage and fetch the cradle. Now Finn and Oonagh's baby had long since left home, so the cradle lay idle in the cupboard. He dragged the cradle into the living room and with them all being giants the cradle almost filled half of the room. Then Oonagh told Finn to take off his clothes and as he protested she told him to just get on with it. Finn stood shivering in his boxer shorts, the ones with the shamrock embroidered in the corner, while Oonagh grabbed a large white towel and folded it into a triangle to make a nappy big enough to fit him. She then found a huge safety pin to secure the giant nappy and told him to climb into the cradle and behave like a baby. Fetching one of her white lacy bonnets, she put it on Finn's fat head and tied it under his whiskery chin in a big bow. Again she instructed him to behave like a baby until she winked at him, then he would know what to do if he used what little brains he had. Mystified and more than a little embarrassed, Finn could only muster 'Goo, goo, goo!' Laughing, Oonagh just grabbed a copper jug and slipped out of the back door.

In the farmyard at the back of the cottage was a lean-to that was home to their one and only cow. Oonagh rather grandly referred to this as her dairy. A large churn contained buttermilk – an ingredient essential for Oonagh's famous soda bread. Filling her copper jug, she grabbed a bag of flour in her other hand and headed back to the kitchen via the house of her neighbour. From the neighbour she asked to borrow twenty griddles and a couple of handfuls of nuts and bolts.

Back in her kitchen, she set to and made twenty farls of soda bread, each with a cast iron griddle in the middle and some containing nuts and bolts. She then made one ordinary one with the letter B (for baby) on the top. She then sat in the rocking chair next to the cradle and just tickled the 'baby's' toes, chuckled and waited …

Before long there was a knocking at the cottage door. Oonagh leapt up, ran to the door and opened it. She was staring straight at the hairy knees of Cuchulain the giant. He told her that he had come to fight the famous giant, Finn McCool. Oonagh told him that Finn was away working on the causeway but that he was welcome to come in and wait to fight Finn when he returned for his supper. Cuchulain ducked his head under the door frame and, entering the small room, saw the cradle with the enormous ugly baby in it. Cuchulain told Oonagh that he'd never seen such an enormous baby. She merely commented that it was a case of 'like father, like son' and asked him if he would like a cup of tea while he waited. The giant confirmed that he would. Oonagh told him that there was a slight problem as Finn hadn't got round to digging a well in their farmyard yet so there wasn't any water for the tea.

Just then a gust of wind blew through the door and shook the whole cottage. Oonagh told the shivering giant that when the wind blew like that Finn normally nipped outside and picked up the cottage and turned it to back into the wind. Perhaps Cuchulain could do that to help her? Cuchulain thought that if Finn could do that, so could he. So he clicked his fingers ten times to give him the strength of twenty giants, and nodding to Oonagh, backed out through the door and, grasping the whole cottage, turned it round so that it backed into the prevailing wind.

Oonagh joined him in the farmyard and pointed to a nearby mountain. She told the giant that in the middle of the mountain there was a spring of water and Finn had been planning to chop it open with one blow so that they could have fresh spring water. Desperate for a cup of tea after his journey from Scotland, Cuchulain clicked his fingers thirteen times to give him the strength of twenty-six giants. He then strode down the hill and with a mighty blow smashed the mountain in two, making a valley with a spring at the bottom, that to this day is still named Glenarm. Oonagh ran down the hill, filled her kettle, and running back up to the cottage placed it on the hob until it was whistling to make tea. As Cuchulain slurped his tea she asked him if he would like something to eat with it.

Ever hungry, the giant told her that he would. She told him that she only had soda bread and warned him that she made her soda bread very heavy and crusty as that was the way that Finn liked it. The giant pronounced that if it was good enough for Finn then it was good enough for him. Hiding a smile, Oonagh handed him one of the special loaves. Snatching the loaf, Cuchulain bit into the bread, smashing five of his teeth on the iron griddle in the middle. He was spitting out broken teeth all over the floor. Oonagh again assured him that the bread was exactly as Finn liked it, but if it was too crusty for him … Furious, Cuchulain again bit into the bread and a couple of the nuts and bolts jammed between his teeth, shearing them clean off.

As the giant spluttered, Oonagh picked up the normal loaf and handed it to the 'baby' who just gratefully gobbled it down. Cuchulain was amazed that a baby could eat bread as hard as that. Oonagh merely invited him to put his finger into the 'baby's' mouth to feel how strong the teeth were. Stupidly Cuchulain did this and, taking her opportunity, Oonagh winked at Finn, who knew exactly what to do, biting the finger clean off and spitting it out like some old sausage.

Cuchulain realised that without the magic middle finger he couldn't double his strength and would be no match for Finn McCool, a man who could turn a house, karate chop a mountain and eat that special soda bread! Ignoring the baby and sloping out of the cottage, he stormed down the hill back towards the sea. In one last gesture of defiance, he took the thunderbolt pancake from his waistcoat pocket and tossed it at the causeway, blowing the wooden walkway to smithereens. Mind you, the hexagonal pillars of rock remain to this day and are known as the Giant's Causeway – and you can visit it. As for Finn and Oonagh, all Finn could do was admit that although he was a great hero, his wife was indeed 'the woman behind the man'. As the two of them settled down to a supper of bacon and cabbage with soda bread and glasses of creamy milk from their 'dairy', Oonagh just smiled modestly.

from
the
kitchen
garden

Part V

FROM THE KITCHEN GARDEN

How to sow beans:
'One for the mouse, one for the crow,
One to rot and one to grow'

The Queen Bee

This story had to be included because when I was a child in the 1950s, my paternal grandfather, who was a stationmaster in the county of Somerset, took me on a day out to a Franciscan friary in Dorset. He met many interesting people in his job and one of them was one of the friars who would travel to meetings or conferences from the station and would often enjoy a chat with my grandfather. This led to Grandfather being invited to visit the friary and he took me with him. The brothers showed me around the vegetable garden where they working before taking me to the beehives and explaining how we get honey, a memorable day. Thanks for all the honey, beekeepers, queen bees and your workers.

This story comes from the Brothers Grimm collection. Their stories are often tricky to tell, as they have been translated from the original versions. It's not an easy step from the printed page to the tongue. I hope I have breathed life into this tale as it contains some of the key elements of European folk tale, namely princes and princesses, a journey, magic and riddles to be solved or tasks to be fulfilled. Enjoy the adventure with the brothers.

Many years ago when birds built their nests in old men's beards there was a castle. This castle was home to a king and his three sons. The two eldest princes were fun-loving mischief-makers and full of bravado. The youngest brother was sensitive, quiet and kind. His father, the king, and his two brothers would sometimes mock him for his soft nature. In doing this they were missing the fact that he was a gentle soul and that in his chest beat a heart of gold.

One day the two eldest princes left home on a quest for adventure and action. When they failed to return after a couple of weeks the king sent the youngest prince to search for them. Although he had never been trusted with such a task before, he was on a mission and after a couple of days he caught up with them. Were they pleased to see him? No they were not. They told him that he would hold them back and ruin their fun. The young prince just rose above their insults and followed them down the road, determined to fulfil the task set by his father.

A little further on the three princes happened upon an ants' nest. The older brother and the middle brother grabbed sticks to stir up the nest and make the ants rush around in fear and panic. The youngest brother told them to leave the ants to bide as they weren't causing any bother. The brothers called him a spoilsport and, disgruntled, continued on their way.

A mile further on the three brothers reached a lake where a line of ducks were swimming by. The middle brother wanted to 'fly' them for fun. The eldest wanted to catch them and cook one for supper. The youngest stopped them, saying that the ducks were far too pretty to eat and didn't need to be frightened into flying, so should be left to swim in peace. Again his brothers told him he was far too soft and they would now go hungry that night as they'd missed their opportunity. As the ducks flew to safety, the three continued their journey.

Then the princes heard a loud buzzing above them and, looking up, noticed a tree with a bee's nest and honey trickling down the trunk. The two older brothers wanted to light a fire and smoke out the bees and steal all of the honey. The younger brother told them that if they left the bees alone they could safely take a handful of honey each for their supper and continue on their way. They managed this without any of them being stung as they had left most of the precious honey for the queen and the worker bees.

A mile or so further down the road they reached a strange-looking castle. This great stone edifice appeared even stranger when they realised the guards, knights and horses that all surrounded the battlements had all been turned to stone. The three princes entered the castle, only to be greeted by a stony silence. They looked around and then noticed a door with a tiny shutter and three locks. The brothers lifted the shutter to discover a small grey man peering at them. Realising that he had visitors, the little man opened the door and led them to a table laden with good food and drink. The princes ate well as the strange little man told them that the castle was under enchantment, a spell that could only be broken if three tasks were accomplished successfully. Sensing an adventure, the princes asked him to reveal the tasks. The little man pointed to a large stone on which the tasks were carved, together with the warning that should they fail, they too would be turned to stone.

The first task was to collect the thousand pearls dropped from the broken necklace of one of the three princesses who had dwelt in the castle. These were scattered in the grass and bushes of the castle grounds. The eldest prince proclaimed that this was an easy task and he rose and set to work. By nightfall he had only found two hundred of the pearls. After he had failed the task there was a flash of light and the eldest brother stood before the others turned to stone.

The middle brother told the youngest one that if the eldest could not complete such a task then he, the youngest, would have no chance at all. So the next day it was the middle brother who set out to find the pearls. By nightfall he had found only another hundred pearls. Having failed, there again was a flash of light and he too was immediately turned to stone.

The youngest prince now realised that the task fell to him. As he knelt among the grass he spotted the Ant King. The tiny creature said to the young prince that as he had been so kind to his colony they had come to help him. The army of ants soon collected all of the remaining pearls to make up the thousand, carrying them on their backs in the way ants transport their eggs. The young prince watched them with delight.

The second task carved on the stone was to collect the key to the princesses' room from the bottom of the lake in the castle grounds. It would have to be collected by sunset. This was a problem for the young prince as his brothers had never allowed him to swim with them and so he had never learnt. As he stood nervously at the water's edge, he caught sight of the ducks swimming towards him. They told him as he had saved their lives they would help him. Diving deep to the bottom, a shining green mallard surfaced with a golden key in his beak. The young prince thanked him and ran to the castle bearing the key. Searching around, he saw a stairway leading up to the top of a tower and, climbing the stairs, he found a wooden door with a golden lock. Using the key, he unlocked the door to discover three sleeping princesses tucked up in their beds.

His third task was to be the toughest. He had to identify which of these princesses was the sweetest. Each had eaten their favourite sweetmeat before going to their beds. The eldest had eaten a spoonful of sugar, the middle one a spoonful of treacle, and the youngest a spoonful of honey. A little of these sweetmeats had remained on their lips.

Gazing at the three, the prince was grappling with the problem when he heard a loud buzzing. The queen bee was circling his head. She told him that as he'd saved her nest she would help him. When she came to land on the lips of the youngest princess she tasted honey and pronounced that this must be the sweetest princess. With this pronouncement came claps of thunder and a lightning storm. With all the tasks completed the enchantment had been ended.

The castle and all in it returned to life, along with the two elder brothers. The elder princes ran to embrace their younger brother, who had saved them. Asking his forgiveness, they promised never again to mock his gentle nature. And as in all happy endings the three princesses and three princes fell in love and married. So the youngest prince and the sweetest princess became king and queen, living in the castle that he had saved from enchantment by his gentle nature and the kindness of his heart.

Jack and the Magic Beans

This is my version of a fairy tale book and pantomime favourite. I always remember that the beans in my grandfather's and father's vegetable gardens were the most successful ones to grow and we would collect and enjoy them together every year. So this story had to be in the collection.

It is enriched with two tiny chapters from 'the library in my mind'. Firstly, the riddle used to entrap Jack is courtesy of my dad, who used it to 'pull my leg' when I was a boy. Secondly, Jack's love song to Daisy the cow was written by Wolverhampton songsmith Bill Caddick for a Christmas show performed by my folk theatre company, Magic Lantern, in the 1970s. I got to play the role of the hen, which thanks to an elaborate costume could lay golden eggs. Thankfully no photos of this have survived the passing years but, sadly, neither have any of the golden eggs!

Jack lived with his mother and they were desperately poor. For supper all they had was 'potatoes and point'. This meant that Jack's mother placed a plate of boiled potatoes on the table and Jack could point at it while imagining how it would taste. This didn't help his hunger, but it did mean the potatoes would last until the next meal. Hungry, all Jack could do was slip out to the shed and seek the comfort of Daisy the cow. Daisy was both his pet and the supplier of a cup of milk for him to dip his crusts in. When things got worse, Jack's mother decided that Daisy would have to be sold to provide money to pay their debts lest they be thrown out of their cottage by their greedy landlord. One day, after a visit from the debt collector, Jack's mother gave him the news he was dreading. Yes, Daisy the cow would have to go. She would be sold to a farmer or even worse! As if that wasn't hard enough for Jack, he was the one who would have to take her and return home with the money. Well at least he would have some choice in finding the cow's new owner, hopefully someone kind and gentle.

With a tear in his eye, Jack put a rope around Daisy's neck and led her off down the road. His mother shouted after him to be sure to get a good price … they needed it. As Jack proudly walked Daisy down the road he sang his little song to her:

> If Daisy was a lady she'd be the one for me
> I'd be as proud as proud could be

As we walked down the street all the folks would sigh
To see little Daisy, pretty little Daisy,
To see little Daisy and I walk by

An old man at the road side didn't 'sigh', he merely noticed a black and white cow led by a boy who seemed a bit simple. Stepping up to Jack, the old man asked him where he was going. Jack told him that he was heading to town to sell his cow for a good price. The old man told him that to get a good price he would need to know how many beans make five. Quickly Jack replied that the answer was 'a bean and a half and half a bean, a bean and a quarter and a quarter bean, half a bean and a whole bean'.

Do you know what, he was right! The old man put his hand in his pocket and pulled out the five beans, telling him that these were the five beans in exchange for his cow.

Jack looked doubtful, so the old man told him that if he planted them in his garden he would discover that they were not just ordinary beans. He said that if Jack was not happy with them after a couple of days then he would give him his cow back. Reluctantly, Jack handed him the rope around the cow's neck, telling him to look after her well. Turning back, Jack headed for home.

Jack arrived home looking very pleased with himself. His mother greeted him, then asked if he'd got a good price for the cow. When Jack handed her the five beans his mother was thrown into a rage, telling him that he was a stupid, stupid boy. She threw the beans out of the window into the garden. Then she sent Jack to bed with a 'flea in his ear'. The following morning Jack was woken by the dawn chorus. The sun had risen but something was casting a shadow over the front of the cottage and his bedroom window. Leaping out of bed and rushing to the window, he was amazed to see that one of the beans had grown into an enormous beanstalk reaching from the garden right up to the sky. It was so high that the top of it was shrouded in clouds. When he woke his mother to show her, she was, if anything, more amazed than Jack. Mother and son stood at the foot of the beanstalk wondering what to do. The solution was easy; Jack was the sort of lad that could not even pass a tree without climbing it. After giving his mother a hug, he wrapped his strong legs around the beanstalk and, grasping it in his hands, he started climbing up towards the clouds. Before long he was climbing through the clouds. Nearing the top of the remarkable beanstalk, Jack saw a path leading through one of the clouds towards a farmhouse. An old woman wearing a bonnet and apron stood in the doorway. She told Jack that he was very brave for tackling such a dangerous climb and asked if he was hungry. Jack, like all young lads, was always hungry. She then asked if he would like some breakfast. Jack was never known to turn down a breakfast. The woman told Jack that he needed to be brave as her husband might soon return and he liked to eat young lads. Leading him into the kitchen, she showed him a safe place to hide behind the stove. As he peeped over the top of the stove he heard heavy footsteps as an ogre stepped into the room. The ogre lifted the lid of the pot bubbling away on the stove and tasted the contents. He obviously had a fierce appetite as, sniffing the air, he chanted:

Fee, fie, foe, fum, I smell the blood of an Englishman
Be he alive or be he dead I'll grind his bones to make my bread.

His wife told him that there was nobody there and that he must be daydreaming. Behind the stove, Jack shook with fear. Peeping out again, Jack saw the woman walk out of the kitchen and then return, handing her husband a basket of golden eggs and quietly passing one to Jack as she walked by. Jack was so surprised he dropped the egg and saw it roll out of the door and drop through a hole in the clouds. The ogre began to count the golden eggs, something he did every time he returned home to check they were all there. He was so engrossed in doing this that Jack seized the opportunity to slip out of the cottage door and race back to the beanstalk and start to climb down.

Down in the garden, Jack's mother had a surprise. Firstly, a golden egg fell down from the clouds, narrowly missing her, then looking upwards she saw Jack's boots and then his breeches as he hastened his descent, fearing he might be chased by the ogre. Jack and his mother met at the bottom of the beanstalk with smiles and hugs. Jack looked up to the top and, seeing no sign of the ogre following him, he told his mother all that had happened and, relieved, they went back into the cottage. With the golden egg Jack and his mother were no longer poor. Smiles returned to their faces and the cottage garden became a happier place. After quite a long time the money Jack and his mother got for selling the golden egg started to run out and Jack knew it was his duty as a loving son to climb back up the beanstalk again.

The next morning Jack reached out of his bedroom window, grasped the beanstalk and started climbing upwards. Once at the top, he looked along the path leading towards the farmhouse and saw the ogre's wife standing in the doorway. She greeted him and told him that if he hid behind the stove she could bring him some breakfast. She warned him that the ogre would soon be back to count his golden eggs. Just then the ground began to shake and Jack began to tremble. The ogre's voice roared out:

Fee, fie, foe, fum, I smell the blood of an Englishman,
Be he alive or be he dead, I'll grind his bones to make my bread.

As the ogre roared out these words the golden cockerel in the farmyard started to crow in fear. The golden hen in the corner of the kitchen started to cluck nervously. The ogre's wife told him that there was nobody there and that all he could smell was the memory of a boy he'd eaten a few days before. The ogre looked doubtful, but he went in to sit and count his golden eggs. The ogre grumbled as he counted; he still had not found the golden egg that had gone missing some time ago and as he counted the remaining eggs his temper grew and his complaining got louder and grumpier. The golden hen started clucking again, fearing for her life. Jack, also fearing for his life, crept out from behind the stove and, grabbing the golden hen, fled outside, running towards the beanstalk. The hen, flapping her wings, escaped from Jack's arms and fluttered down through the hole in the clouds, landing in Jack's garden. There was another surprise for Jack's mother as, landing at her feet, the hen laid a golden egg. She was even more delighted when Jack climbed down into their garden. Jack was relieved that, looking up to the top of the beanstalk, there was neither sight nor sound of the ogre, and told his mother of his adventure.

The hen laid a golden egg every day, so life once again was good for Jack and his mother … until one day the hen just stopped laying. Jack and his mother tried to work out why this should be. Then Jack's mother realised that the golden hen must be missing the company of the golden cockerel. Jack knew that he must once again set off up the beanstalk. At the top of the beanstalk, Jack once again walked towards the farmhouse. The golden cockerel, in its usual pride of place on top of the midden, crowed loudly. This woke the ogre and warned him that they had visitors. He stormed down the stairs, chanting:

Fee, fie, foe, fum, I smell the blood of an Englishman,
Be he alive or be he dead, I'll grind his bones to make my bread.

Scuttling behind him, his wife tried to convince her husband that there was nobody there, and seeing Jack slip into the kitchen behind them, she whispered to him to hide in the big copper jam pan behind the stove. Jack managed to do this without the ogre spotting him. The ogre started to sniff around the kitchen and in a sulk told his wife that one of his eggs was missing as well as his golden hen and that he was not going to let anything else be taken from him. His wife knew what might calm his temper and went to fetch his golden harp. As soon as the magic harp began to play a lullaby, Jack, peering out of the jam pan, saw the ogre's head begin to nod as he fell into a deep sleep. As soon as the ogre was snoring asleep, Jack leapt out of the jam pan, shot across the kitchen and out of the door. Running across the farmyard, he managed to grab the golden cockerel from its roost and, with a firm grip of it in his arms, headed towards the beanstalk. He soon heard the thump, thump, thump of heavy footsteps behind him. The ogre had woken when Jack had run past the golden harp, knocked it over and it had stopped playing. Now the ogre was chasing after him. Jack was young and fast and, still gripping the cockerel, was already halfway down the beanstalk before the ogre arrived at the top.

In the garden Jack's mother was pleased to see him back safe and, grabbing the cockerel, put him down by the golden hen, who clucked happily to see him again. Looking up, Jack and his mother saw the ogre's boots and then his breeches as he descended closer to them. Jack rushed to the garden shed and, taking the biggest axe they had, ran back to chop down the beanstalk. Swinging the axe, in three mighty blows the giant plant began to keel over. The ogre had a spectacular fall. He hit the ground so hard that with his great weight he created a hole big enough to completely consume him from the tip of his toes to the top of his head. Indeed, the ogre was never seen again. As for Jack and his mother, they lived in comfort for the rest of their lives:

> Now Jack and his mother are happy, so are we
> Let's put on the kettle and have a cup of tea.

The Parsley Queen

The heart and soul of every kitchen garden is the herb patch. Freshly chopped herbs can enliven even a bland dish.

When a member of the upper classes or aristocracy becomes queen of the land it is not a surprise. However, if a peasant girl is elevated to that role then there's a story worth telling. This is especially true if this change of status is facilitated by a common herb that has pride of place in the kitchen garden.

Although this story was seeded in the Far East, it has many of the motifs that are also found in Western folk tales.

Many years ago in a faraway land there lived a poor couple. Late in life this husband and wife had a child, a daughter so precious to them that they called her their 'little princess'. Sad it is to tell that while the daughter was but a young girl, on the cusp of becoming a young woman, her father took ill and looked likely to die. Being loving and caring, the daughter tended to her father, becoming increasingly distressed as his pain and discomfort increased. He confided in his daughter that, although he had no fear of death, the only thing that worried him was that someone needed to take care of his wife after his death. The dutiful girl assured her father that she would continue to love and look after his wife for him. Safe in the knowledge that his daughter would care for her mother, the old man could now be at peace and not long after allowed himself to slip out of this life.

After a time spent grieving, the mother and daughter settled down to their life together. Whatever the calls upon her time and energy, the young girl would always put her mother's wishes and needs above her own. They loved sharing their time in the kitchen together for the mother was a fine cook and even more adept at passing on her recipes and skills to her daughter. The old woman particularly loved to use fresh herbs to enhance the food she prepared. This was back in the day when most of the herbs that we now plant and grow in the kitchen garden were foraged from the wild. The herb most favoured by the mother was parsley, which she used in sauces, salads and savoury dishes.

Now it just happened that one day the girl's mother sent her out with a basket to gather wild parsley. The young girl was in the middle of the field picking the parsley and diligently filling her basket when a mighty procession could be seen making its way down the road by the field that she was in. It was in fact the prince of the land, who was accompanied by a large entourage of his courtiers. This procession was so grand that all the villagers ran from their houses and surrounding fields to view the spectacle and cheer their prince. Enjoying hearing the cheering, the prince looked out of his carriage and gave a royal wave to his subjects, who bowed low to show him the respect they felt for him. The young girl seemed unaware of this excitement. She was engrossed in her work, for nothing was ever more important to her than fulfilling the chores and wishes of her mother and so keeping her promise to her father. Gazing around the scene, the prince noticed the beautiful young girl still working. He wondered why she had not stopped and run to the roadside to join the excitement. He sent his most trusted servant over to the field the girl was in to ask her why she had worked on and not been moved by the splendour of the occasion as all the other villagers had been. The young girl told the servant of the promise made to her dying father and the duty of care she felt for her widowed mother. When the servant relayed this back to the prince, far from being offended at being ignored, the prince seemed impressed by the love and loyalty the peasant girl had for her family.

Halting the procession, the prince ordered some of his servants to help the girl fill the basket and bring her back to join him in his carriage. Without further ado the delighted prince and a rather surprised peasant girl made their way back along the road to the girl's cottage to deliver the basket of parsley to her mother. The mother was taken aback at the arrival of a royal procession outside her home. The prince told the girl to present the basket of parsley to her mother and then bring her over to his carriage to speak with him. He told the girl's mother of how impressed he was by the loyalty and love she had shown for her and that she was indeed lucky to have such a fine daughter. He then ordered the procession to continue on its way.

In the days and months that followed, the prince made sure that his journeys from the palace always took him along the road past the cottage of the young girl and her mother, and he always made sure to stop and speak to the girl who had so impressed him. In time he realised that he was in love with the young girl and eventually made her his queen with the promise that he would agree that they would always take care of her mother.

When the folk of the land spread the story of how this royal couple had first met, they fondly named her the 'Parsley Queen'.

Soup for a Saint

Living in an era of TV dinners and laptop food, one occasion where people are more likely to sit down together for a family meal is Christmas. As a storyteller and lover of food who thinks and works seasonally, it is my pleasure to include in this collection a tale that you can delight in sharing with your nearest and dearest at Christmas time.

It was the east wind from Russia that brought this story to these islands, together with this hearty beetroot soup. Savour both the story and the soup.

Many years ago there was a hotel in Russia famous for its food and hospitality. The hotel owner was rich and popular. It was the iron winter and the snow was so deep you could almost lean on it. Every room in the hotel was prepared for a guest and there was a big pot of soup bubbling on the hob, but no travellers could get there. The hotel owner was rattling around the big empty building, alone. As the clock ticked towards midnight, there was a knocking on the heavy oak door. As the hotelier opened the door, he discovered a tramp, an old man with bright blue eyes, a long white beard and a ragged red coat. The tramp begged for a bite to eat and a bed for the night. The hotel owner told him that he could 'just about squeeze him in', but that it would cost him three roubles. The tramp turned out his pockets to show they were empty and told the hotel owner he had no money, but would pay the debt as soon as he could. If he wasn't helped he would surely perish in the snow.

The hotel owner took pity on the tramp, leading him into the warm hotel and sitting him on a big wooden chair by the fire. He brought the starving old man a big steaming bowl of borscht – beetroot soup – with a twist of sour cream and half a loaf of rye bread. The tramp devoured the soup greedily. It was the first food he'd had for more than a week. In fact, he ate it so hungrily that the beetroot left a red stain on his white moustache. He wiped his mouth with the back of his hand, thanking the hotelier for his kindness and again repeating his promise to pay as soon as he could. He would be leaving first thing in the morning.

After a good night's sleep in a comfortable bed, the tramp was up and away with the first light of day. Seeing the footprints in the snow disappearing up the road, the hotelier thought he would never see the three roubles he was owed.

Strangely, that very day the snow melted and folk could again travel to the hotel. Trade picked up and the hotel owner felt he wanted to go to the cathedral to say a prayer of thanks for his new-found luck.

He walked the twenty miles to Moscow city, to the great cathedral. As he walked through the gate to the city walls, the cathedral bells rang. Up the stone steps the hotelier went and opened the great wooden doors of the church. The walls of the cathedral were covered with icons, beautiful paintings of the saints, decorated with real gold leaf. One painting, diagonally across the nave, drew the hotelier towards it. It was a picture of an old man with a long white beard, bright blue eyes and a ragged red coat, a man strangely familiar to him. He couldn't help but notice that along the bottom of the white moustache was a red beetroot stain. It was indeed the image of the old man he had helped the previous night. He decided to say his prayer in front of that picture. He bought a candle and stooped to press it in the shallow sand tray in front of the picture. The candle bumped against something. Flicking the sand away with his fingers, he discovered three rouble coins. The old tramp had kept his promise. Pocketing the coins, the hotelier finished his prayer and looked at the icon for one last time. At the base of the picture were two words written: the name of the old man.

Those two words read St Nicholas. In Russia he is called St Nicholas but we know him as Father Christmas.

Many families leave a mince pie and a sherry to welcome Father Christmas. Now you know this tale you might choose to leave him a small bowl of his favourite soup, borscht, with a twist of sour cream of course.

A Pumpkin for the Party

All seasonal festivals are in some way linked to seasonal food. The seasonal festival that has grown exponentially is Halloween. While this growth has come from the US custom of 'Trick or Treat', fed by their culture of shock/horror movies, the British Halloween involving apple bobbing, apple-on-the-line, and turnip lanterns is more linked to our seasonal harvest celebrations. In this way we become closer to healthy fruit and vegetable dishes than to 'tooth rot' sweets. However, 'moderation in all things' might be our watchword when it comes to pumpkin pie.

Everybody loves a good party, especially if the food is good.

There was once a friendly witch who hosted the best Halloween parties in the world. The reason she gave the best Halloween parties in the world was because she made the best pumpkin pie in the whole wide world. Her parties and her pie were so popular that she had to start making pies long in advance and store them in her pantry. So keen was she that she began to think about Halloween as summer was drawing to a close.

One year she went to buy a large pumpkin before the end of summer and the shopkeeper smiled and told her that she was earlier than ever. He told her that if she peeled and chopped the pumpkin the following day, ready to make her pies, before she put the peel and rubbish into the bin she should take one seed and plant it in some fertile soil. With a little sun and rain, he said, a pumpkin would grow for her to pick and hollow out when Halloween came round to make a pumpkin lantern with a candle in the middle. The friendly witch listened well and, thanking the shopkeeper, turned and lugged the large orange pumpkin home.

She prepared her pastry and then peeled, chopped and cooked the flesh with sugar and spices to make the filling. As she collected the bits she didn't need for the bin, she chose one large seed and wondered where would be the most fertile soil to plant it. After much consideration, she decided that the best place would be the churchyard, for wasn't the soil made richer by all the corpses that had been buried there for hundreds of years? She wasn't scared to go to the churchyard as it was a peaceful place. Clutching the seed, she arrived there while there was just enough light to see what she was doing. She made a hole in the soil and planted the seed on a mound.

She headed home and washed her hands, and then baked her pie before making her invitations and deciding on her guest list. That was easy. She used the same guest list every year! She always sent invitations to her very best friends: the silver witch, the wizard, the little devil, the skeleton and the little black cat.

While she waited for their replies, she would have time to design Halloween decorations for her little cottage. She made card pumpkins and white skull paper chains for the walls, ghosts made of white netting for the windows, and pyramids of papier mâché apples for the tables. Then she had to contain her excitement as she waited for the magic day of Halloween. All of her guests had replied, thanking her for the invite and saying they would love to come.

When the wonderful day eventually came round, the friendly witch was hopping around with excitement. She brought out the pumpkin pies and waited. The first to arrive was her best friend, the silver witch, followed soon after by the wizard hovering just above the ground. How he frowned as he was cold from his journey round. The friendly witch told them to warm their bones by the fireside. Then there was a strange rattling sound as the 'skelly' opened the door with a bony hand and danced in. Before too long there was a clap of thunder and a flash of lightning as the little devil appeared in the room. However, there was no sign of the little black cat; it was always fashionably late.

The assembled friends all suggested that it was about time for a slice of the legendary pumpkin pie. The friendly witch told her guests that before they could eat they had to go with her to the graveyard. Shivering and shaking with fear, they told her that only a crazy person would go to the graveyard in the dark at Halloween. She told them that there was nothing to be afraid of there, as if the people hadn't harmed them when they were alive, then they wouldn't harm them when they were dead. The friends nodded in agreement and, following in line, headed out of the cottage and down to the graveyard.

In the shadow of the church tower on a mound of earth, the group discovered an enormous bright orange pumpkin. As they stood around the pumpkin, the friendly witch grabbed hold of it and:

> She pulled and she tugged as hard as she could
> But the pumpkin just stood.

The friendly witch looked round for help and the silver witch held on to the friendly witch and the friendly witch held on to the pumpkin, so together:

> They pulled and they tugged as hard as they could
> But the pumpkin just stood.

More help was needed, so the wizard hovered forward. The wizard held on to the silver witch, the silver witch held on to the friendly witch and the friendly witch held on to the pumpkin and:

> They pulled and they tugged as hard as they could
> But the pumpkin just stood.

With a rattle and a clatter, the skelly's bony hand grabbed the wizard. The wizard held on to the silver witch, the silver witch held on to the friendly witch and the friendly witch held on to the pumpkin and:

They pulled and they tugged as hard as they could
But the pumpkin just stood.

With a shower of sparks, the little devil grabbed the skelly. The
'skelly' held on to the wizard, the wizard held on to the silver
witch, the silver witch held on to the friendly witch and the
friendly witch held on to the pumpkin and:

They pulled and they tugged as hard as they could
But the pumpkin just stood.

Whatever could they do? The friends were cold and hungry.
Just then, a stroke of luck, who should turn up but the little
black cat. Purring an apology for being late, the little black cat
was keen to help. So the little black cat held on to the little
devil, the little devil held on to the skelly, the skelly held on
to the wizard, the wizard held on to the silver witch, the silver
witch held on to the friendly witch, and the friendly witch
held on to the pumpkin and:

They pulled and they tugged, nobody grumbled
And the pumpkin broke free and over they tumbled.

Lying giggling in a heap, with nobody hurt, the friends jumped
up and shook themselves off. Then in a line following the
friendly witch holding the pumpkin, they danced back to the
cottage for pie and party games. Together they hollowed out
the enormous pumpkin, carving a scary face on it, and with a
candle lit inside they had made their Halloween lantern. As
they cleared up the waste, they knew that there was one thing
they had to do. They had to save at least one of the seeds to

plant and grow a pumpkin so that they could do it all over again the following year.

A relative of 'The Enormous Turnip' story, within my version of the story is the recipe for your family or community Halloween celebration with games, craft activities, fun and food. Happy Halloween!

The Princess of Turnips

Although the bones of the story that follows is another courtesy of the Brothers Grimm, the 'sack of knowledge' section of the tale has such a rich vein of nonsense that I couldn't resist embroidering it with my favourite 'patter' from the Quack Doctor's speech in just about every mummers' play I have ever heard or performed in. It also elevates the role of a humble turnip soup to a soup fit for a king.

I doubt whether Jacob and Wilhelm will be turning in their graves!

Many years ago in far Bavaria there lived two brothers who served as soldiers. Now it just happened that one of the brothers was very rich and the other very poor. One day the poorer brother, who had a plot of land the size of a pocket handkerchief, decided it was time to change his fortune. Walking to his tiny barn at the bottom of his field, he took off his soldier's jacket and hung it from a nail on the wooden beam. Resting his spade and hoe on his shoulder, he walked purposefully out to the field and started digging and hoeing. He thought the answer to his problems lay in the soil. He was now a farmer.

The winter had ended; the season was right. He had saved turnip seeds, which he sprinkled into a furrow in the rich soil. To his delight the sun and the rain did their work and soon green shoots appeared. These shoots started to form bulbous roots, which grew daily. For some reason one of these plants grew bigger, stronger and faster than all the others. It became apparent to this young man that in this turnip he had grown something special, a magnificent monster of a vegetable.

On his travels as a soldier he had heard of how in other lands they had claimed to grow turnips so big that the locals could hollow them out to use as barns for their cattle or even as homes for themselves! The young brother's turnip looked as if it might be even bigger than the ones he'd heard of, and that wouldn't be a lie! The turnip continued to grow.

Rather than being the answer to the young man's problems, it presented him with a bigger one. What was he to do with it? He thought that if he sold it he would never get its true worth. He could eat it, but two small ones would probably taste better. Local folk walking by and marvelling as they passed under the shadow cast by this enormous white root had christened it the 'Princess of Turnips'. Aware of this, the young farmer thought the only decent thing for him to do was to take this princess as a present to the king. This was quite a difficult task as it would need two oxen and a cart. Nevertheless, the farmer set out to make his way to the castle.

He presented the Princess of Turnips to the king, who told him he was one of the luckiest men in the world to grow something that special. The farmer told the king that it was to the contrary as he was very poor and indeed it was his elder brother who was the lucky one as he had a large house, much land and great wealth.

The king told the younger brother that for his generosity he would give him land, cattle and gold to equal his brother. The young man thanked the king and, placing the gold in his oxcart, headed home.

When his brother heard of what had happened at the castle he was immediately jealous. He reckoned that if he took gifts that had more worth than a vegetable to the king then his reward would be even bigger than that received by his brother. The next day, driving a pair of his finest horses and bearing bags of gold and silver, the older brother made his way to the castle. On accepting these gifts the king smiled and stated that the older brother might like a princess as a gift in return. Then he gave the older brother the most precious thing that he owned … the 'Princess of Turnips'. The older brother was furious. Of course, it was polite to thank the king and take the enormous vegetable home. On this journey he became angrier and angrier; he was trying to dream up a way to get his own back on his younger brother.

The next day he engaged the services of a gang of murderers. He instructed them to hide in the bushes near the great oak tree on the forest track. He sent a message to his brother that he had heard there was treasure to be had under the great oak and that they should meet up together there, dig the treasure and share it. Ever trusting, the young brother failed to 'smell a rat'. When he arrived at the great oak there was no sign of his brother. Carrying out the instructions of the older brother, the murderous gang leapt out of the bushes, bound the younger brother and, forcing him into a sack, hauled him up to the top of the tree. Just then the gang heard the clip clopping of hooves, a shout and cheery singing. Someone was approaching. In fear for their lives, the ruffians took to their heels and ran. High up in the sack our hero also heard the sound of a possible helper approaching. He worked hard on the top of the sack, forcing a hole big enough to pop his head out. On a beautiful stallion riding up to the tree was an intelligent-looking young man, in fact a student of medicine. Our hero called down. The student was wary; he knew there were rogues and robbers in that area and this might be an ambush. He shouted to our hero, asking what he was doing up there in a sack.

From on high our hero shouted back, telling him that he was hiding in the Sack of Knowledge, a centre of learning far greater than any university. Mystified, the student asked him whatever he meant. Our hero shouted back that in that sack he could gain knowledge about every country in the world. He himself had learned about, 'Italy Sicily, France and Spain, Russia, Prussia and Ukraine'. Not only that, he had learnt enough medical knowledge to cure every known disease. He knew how to cure 'The ips, the pips, the palsy and the gout, pains within and pains without. He could even cure a ruptured spleen and rid all of Covid 19!' The student fancied a shortcut to all this knowledge and asked if he might be allowed to avail himself of some time in the sack acquiring some of it. Our hero agreed and so the student lowered the sack to the ground. As the student dismounted from his horse, our hero helped him into the sack, pulled the top tight and hoisted him up to the top of the great tree. Then he mounted the student's fine white stallion and rode it home to join the horses gifted to him by the king in exchange for the 'Princess of Turnips'. An hour or so later he sent one of his new servants to release the young student and bring him back for a fine supper of creamy turnip soup. Mind you, he didn't invite his older brother to join them. In fact, he never set eyes on him ever again. Perhaps he had learnt something from the Sack of Knowledge after all.

Part V

FROM SEA & SHORE

You shall have a fishy on a little dishy,
You shall have a fishy when the boat comes in.

Why the Sea is Salty

This tale explains how we have come to have sea salt to add flavour to our dishes! The tale has many variants in Scandinavia, however the bones of my version come from one of my mentors, Scots traveller Duncan Williamson. I have affectionately located it in Whitby, a seaside town I love. I dedicate it to my friends from the Whitby lifeboat crew and the memory of Mollie Grove, the 'Duchess of Whitby'. Mollie loved my riddles so I begin the story with one of them.

> Torn from the land
> Fruit of the sea
> Dinner is dull unless you pinch me.

Down in the fires of hell things were not going well. Old Nick, Old Scratch, the devil himself, was bored. Magog, his mother, knew that there was nothing worse for a mother to deal with than a bored son. He was stomping around the fire in a temper, kicking cinders and sparks into the air. Above the fire on a mantelshelf stood a strange-looking object, a salt mill given to him by his favourite uncle. It had been one of his most loved toys and he would often pause to stroke its smooth wooden shape. Magog leaned over the fire and took the salt mill from the shelf when her son wasn't looking. She wrapped it into her black shawl and began to climb the long ladder up to the Earth's surface.

Stepping off the top of the ladder, she found that she was standing on the quayside of the small port of Whitby. In these times a circle of fishing boats are moored around the quay, but in those days it was a circle of square-rigged sailing ships. Some of these were whaling ships and some trading vessels ready to travel the world exporting and importing goods. A three-masted trader was moored with its gangplank stretched over to the quay, awaiting the arrival of the captain and crew, who were enjoying a last visit to a harbour-side inn.

Opposite this large ship was an old curiosity shop. The owner of the shop was a man who would sometimes sail the world in search of goods he would acquire from poor peasants to bring back and sell to visitors for a much higher price, making a huge profit for himself. Magog strode into this old shop and the doorbell rang. The shop owner was behind the counter packing his kitbag, for that very day he was to board the waiting ship to acquire more stock. Hearing the doorbell, he rose up and found himself facing a tiny old woman wearing a black shawl. When he enquired what she wanted, Magog produced the wooden salt mill with the little metal wheel on top. The shop owner told her in no uncertain terms that he didn't want to buy anything from her, or anybody else for that matter. Magog told him that the unusual salt mill was not for sale but that it was a gift. She told him that if he said the words 'salt mill give me salt' the wheel would turn and crystals of salt would pour out of it, even if it had not been filled beforehand. With that the little old woman turned out of the shop and was gone. With a shrug the shop owner stuffed the salt mill into his kitbag and, locking his shop door, threw the kit bag over his shoulder and walked up the gang plank of the waiting ship. Two rough-looking sailors pulled up the plank and the ship set sail.

Climbing back down the ladder to the fires of hell, Magog became aware that things had got even worse. The devil was in a filthy temper. He screamed at his mother that he was even more bored as he had no new souls to torment. Most of the people dying were the good ones and they were all going to heaven. Even worse, someone had stolen his favourite toy, the magic salt mill. If he could only catch the thief he would impale them on his trident and toast them over the fire. His mother told him that it was she who had taken the mill, but that she had a cunning plan and had done it for his own good. Furious, he told her to bend over and was just about to jab the points of the trident into her bottom when she begged him to give her twenty-four hours for her plan to work.

Out in the North Sea, the shop owner was not enjoying a happy voyage. The hundred sailors on board were drunkards and rough and foul-mouthed. The captain was unpleasant in the extreme. He was all too handy with his cat-o'-nine-tails and, although he had a loyal wife back home, whenever they were in port he would be off with 'ladies of the night'. Together with the greedy shop owner, on board were one hundred and two wicked men. At supper time, planks were placed on barrels to serve as tables. All they would have to eat was 'tattie' soup and 'weevily' biscuits. The soup was so thin the captain could read the chart through it.

The sailors never complained about the weevils, for that was their meat ration! One moaning sailor said it would be more edible if they only had some salt. The cook, who didn't like being moaned at, said that there was no salt. With a smile, the shop owner reached into his kitbag and produced the salt mill. The cook repeated that he had no salt to put in it. Triumphantly the shop owner said 'salt mill give me salt' and the tiny wheel began to turn. Perfect crystals of shining white salt started to pour out of the wooden mill, so they could all take a pinch and sprinkle it into their soup. Before long the pile of salt was waist deep. The shop owner realised that he didn't know how to stop it. The captain ordered the crew to leave their food and start shovelling the salt below deck. The wheel continued to turn and before long the pile of salt was mast high. The captain told them that the ship was now top-heavy and if the weather worsened they would be in trouble. No sooner had he said that than the wind started to freshen, an easterly. Soon they were in the teeth of a gale. The first huge wave capsized the ship and she sank to the bottom with the loss of all one hundred and two men. Being wicked men, they all went straight to hell.

By the fire twenty-four hours had passed and the devil was again preparing to toast his mother. He was just about to do this when through the gates arrived one hundred and two fresh souls for him to torment. They were placed in cages for his imps to prod with their pointed sticks. The devil threw his trident down, for hadn't his mother's cunning plan worked?

As for that shipwreck, it's still on the ocean bed and do you know, the wheel on that salt mill is still turning. If you do not believe me, the next time you are at the seaside, just dip your finger in the sea and taste it – it's salty! So that is why the sea is salty and we have sea salt to flavour our food.

Shrimps for a Giant

In 1999, when telling stories in the town of Ulverston as a guest of the Furness Traditions Festival, I was approached in the café by a family who had enjoyed my stories and asked if I had a story especially for them. I asked where they were from and they replied that they lived and worked in the village of Flookburgh as shrimp pickers, just as their forebears had. Delving into my repertoire and drawing on any knowledge I had of Morecambe Bay, I told them the story that follows. They went away delighted. I hope both the tale and the prospect of potted shrimps for tea will also delight you.

A giant came from Scotland to Lakeland. The locals, on seeing his arrival, were terrified of him, partly because he was huge but mainly because he was Scottish! Tired from his journey, the giant looked for somewhere to sit and rest. Near where the town of Ulverston now stands he came across a hill and realised that if he sat on top of this hill he could paddle his left foot in Morecambe Bay and his right foot in the Duddon Estuary.

Sitting on the hill and peering over Morecambe Bay, the giant saw something he had never seen before. Where he had come from in Scotland there were fishermen on the coast, but they all fished from boats with nets and lines. The fishermen of Morecambe Bay, however, didn't need boats. They were using nets and lines but as the tide went out so far they could use heavy horses to tow their nets. However, there are very dangerous parts of the Bay where patches of floating sand, known as quicksand, can suck an animal or a person under and drown them. In the old days entire coaches and horses sometimes disappeared in the sands of the Bay.

One of the local fishermen was Joss Westmorland. Joss trawled for shrimps using two heavy horses, a chestnut and a grey, named Chalk and Cheese. Joss and his wife lived on a farm close to the 'Guide over Sands' pub. Joss knew well the treacherous nature of the Bay and could steer his horses between these deadly patches of sinking sand. However, on this particular day Joss drove Chalk and Cheese a little too close to a patch of quicksand. Both horses started to sink, followed by the trawl and, of course, Joss, who had two hand-turns of the reins. In a matter of minutes both the horses and the fisherman were up to their chins in sand and water.

Back at the farmhouse, Joss's wife sensed danger. She went out into the yard and put the spyglass to her eye. She saw her husband, his horses and the trawl sinking fast. She feared that before the evening she would be a widow. On the hill, the giant also sensed the danger. He put his hand to his forehead and, seeing the trouble, stood up and then took three great steps into the Bay. Each step was a mile long. Bending down, he picked up the horses and the net, which was full of shrimps, in his right hand. At the same time, he picked up the fisherman in his left. The giant placed them safely back in their yard at the farm before sitting back on his hill with the net full of shrimps to eat.

The giant had saved Morecambe Bay's favourite fisherman so the local people weren't frightened of him anymore. Now that giant's name was Angus Hoad, so ever since that hill has been called Hoad Hill, and if you don't believe me consult your Ordnance Survey map and there you will find Hoad Hill. So it must be true! Also, to thank the giant, every week local folk brought him a net full of shrimps to eat.

The Grasmere Gingerbread Man

On the Cumbrian coast, not far from Grasmere, stands the port of Whitehaven. From around the sixteenth century this port was involved in trade with the Caribbean and even became the third largest port in Britain. Spices, unrefined sugars and rum were brought to the port and soon became ingredients in the food of the region. Popular in Cumbria were such delights as Westmorland pepper cake, Cumberland Rum Nicky tart and, of course, gingerbread. Not all gingerbread is baked in squares, as you will discover in this next tale!

As a storyteller I have the freedom to move from fact to fiction and from fiction to fantasy. Within a tale my characters can time travel at will, without rhyme or reason. So it is that, in my version of the well-known tale that follows, while the places mentioned still exist in the village that is home to my Storyteller's Garden, the protagonists in the story lived in the village at different times. You, as the reader, can decide whether they have come together as ghosts or as figments of the storyteller's imagination.

Opposite the Storyteller's Garden is the tiny cottage where the best gingerbread in the world is still being made. Enjoy the story and then cross the road to visit Sarah Nelson's unique Gingerbread Shop, right next to the church in the Lakeland village of Grasmere.

A shepherd's cottage stood at Greenhead Ghyll in the Lakeland village of Grasmere, near the foot of Dunmail Raise. Times past this was the home of an old shepherd, his wife and family. Their children had long since grown up and left home, drawn to the city as is sometimes the way with youngsters in rural communities. So the shepherd and his wife were 'empty nesters', but still enjoyed each other's company. The shepherd continued to work hard, enjoying being with his dog and the sheep. His wife, in her stead, was a busy and accomplished cook.

One evening the shepherd was out at a 'meet' at the nearby Travellers' Rest Inn. On entering the pub his friends called upon him to sing a song, for that's the way it is at a shepherd's meet. After enjoying a hearty bowl of 'tatie pot', he stood up and sang:

> Our children have taken the road to the cities
> And strangers have come with eyes open wide.
> But will they remember the life that existed
> when the last Lakeland fellsman has died?

Back at the cottage, the shepherd's wife set to with the baking. Mixing together flour, eggs, ground ginger, butter, sugar and milk, she stirred up a rich gingerbread mix. Remembering times past when around her ankles was the patter of her children's feet, she didn't press her mixture into a baking tray, choosing rather to fashion it into the shape of a small man, which she stood on the tray. Then she placed the tray into the oven for about twenty minutes. This done, she sat in her armchair until she heard the sound of her husband heading home up the track. Opening the cottage door, he could smell the wonderful aroma of baking gingerbread and ran up to his wife to give her a hug, for he loved the gingerbread she made, but in his haste he forgot to shut the door. Just then there was a knocking from inside the oven and he looked at the oven door and then looked towards his wife. The shepherd's wife assured him that he hadn't imagined it, for she had heard the knocking as well. She opened the oven door and 'boing!' in a glorious puff of ginger-sweet smell, out jumped a little gingerbread man singing:

Run, run as fast as you can
You can't catch me, I'm the Gingerbread Man.

Grabbing his shepherd's crook, the old man and his wife gave chase as the Gingerbread Man headed out of the open door and down the hill towards the village. So heading down the hill was the Gingerbread Man, chased by the old shepherd waving his crook and his wife.

At the bottom of the hill they spotted a man heading along the road towards Grasmere with a large roll of fine tweed across his shoulders. It was Mickey Mosscrop, known as old Tweedie, as he regularly brought fine tweed cloth from the borders to be sold in Grasmere. Despite the weight on his back, when he saw the Gingerbread Man he joined in the chase as it headed towards the forge further along the road. It was a forge well placed to serve passing coaches and horses with repairs and reshoeing. So heading towards the forge was the Gingerbread Man chased by the old shepherd waving his crook, his wife, and old Tweedie lugging his roll of cloth as again the Gingerbread Man sang:

Run, run as fast as you can,
You can't catch me , I'm the Gingerbread Man.

The blacksmith looked up from his anvil where he was hammering a red hot horseshoe, which he gripped in long iron tongs. Twirling the tongs, the blacksmith joined the chase as the Gingerbread Man headed over White Bridge and into the centre of the village. So heading towards the church was the Gingerbread Man chased by the old shepherd waving his crook, his wife, old Tweedie bearing his roll of tweed and the blacksmith twirling his iron tongs.

As they neared the church again the Gingerbread man sang:

> Run, run as fast as you can,
> You can't catch me, I'm the Gingerbread Man.

Now next door to St Oswald's church was a tiny stone building called Gate Cottage, that had once been the home of the little school in Grasmere. However, times change and the village found it needed a bigger building as its school, so the school was now in its new home by the River Rothay. With the tiny cottage now empty, it became home to a local cook and baker, Sarah Nelson, and her husband Wilfred, the grave digger for the church. Living and baking in this tiny cottage, Sarah sold her gingerbread from a tree stump next to the church. The glorious smell attracted the children on their way home from school and didn't it amuse them that these delights were coming from the building that was the old school. Sarah was always pleased to see them and to help them learn to read and write would make gingerbread in the shape of letters of the alphabet. If the children could recognise the letter, then they could eat it. Now that's motivational education.

As a group of children were just claiming their gingerbread letters there was a commotion as towards them raced the Gingerbread Man, followed by the old shepherd waving his crook, his wife, old Tweedie bearing his roll of tweed and the blacksmith twirling his iron tongs. The school children scoffing their gingerbread letters, Sarah shaking her wooden spoon and Wilfred the grave digger swinging his spade, all joined in the chase as they headed towards Town End, and again the Gingerbread Man sang:

Run, run as fast as you can
You can't catch me I'm the Gingerbread Man.

At Town End, in the garden of Dove Cottage, who should they find but a poet who always gave his words' worth! He was just completing a poem with his quill quivering as his sister, Dorothy, stood by him with an armful of daffodils she'd come across as inspiration. As the crowd passed by and turned towards the lake shore, they couldn't resist joining in. So heading towards the lake was the Gingerbread Man, chased by the old shepherd waving his crook, his wife, old Tweedie still struggling with his roll of cloth, the blacksmith twirling his iron tongs, the school children scoffing their gingerbread letters, Sarah shaking her wooden spoon, Wilfred the grave digger swinging his spade, William the poet quivering his quill and Dorothy carefully clutching her daffodils as the Gingerbread Man sang for the last time:

Run, run as fast as you can
You can't catch me, I'm the Gingerbread Man.

Who should be stood on the lake shore but old Daddy Fox, who had just outrun the hounds of the Coniston hunt and, seeing the Gingerbread Man was in a similar plight, invited him to jump on his back. The fox paddled out into the lake and started swimming towards the island. The water splashed up and the fox knew that there was nothing worse than soggy gingerbread, so he invited the Gingerbread Man to jump up on to his head as he continued swimming. Still the water splashed up, so the fox invited the Gingerbread Man to balance on the end of his nose. Ooh, the gingerbread did smell good. As old Daddy Fox paddled ashore at the island he felt hungry and could resist the temptation no more. So he tossed the Gingerbread Man up into the air, caught him in his jaws and gobbled him all up.

On the far shore all the people who had been chasing were shaking their fists. There was the old shepherd, with his crook by his side, and his wife sitting on the lake shore, old Tweedie sitting resting on top of his roll of cloth, the blacksmith exhausted standing with his iron tongs laid at his feet, the school children scoffing the last few crumbs of gingerbread, Sarah putting her wooden spoon back into her pinny pocket, Wilfred the grave digger leaning on his spade, William holding his quill and dreaming up his next poem and Dorothy gathering up the daffodils that she had dropped during the chase.

After a short rest all they could do was to turn and slowly make their way back through the village to their homes. To this day a Gingerbread Man has never again been seen running through the village of Grasmere, but you can still go to Sarah Nelson's cottage by the church to sample the best gingerbread in the world.

Stargazey Pie

The Cornish have always boasted a fine bill of fare, which includes early fruits and vegetables and, of course, the 'fruits of the sea'.

Back in the 1970s in my shadow puppet company Magic Lantern's van, I was hurtling along a Belgian auto route to our next show when a beeping car drew alongside. In the passenger seat I recognised the smiling face of Brenda Wooton, a.k.a. Mama Cornwall. Winding down the window, she signalled to me to do likewise and, leaning out of her window, with all the skill of a relay runner, she passed me an enormous Cornish pasty. 'That'll keep you going until you get to Brussels,' she shouted. When we met later at the same gig she sang a song about a tiny Cornish fishing village sharing food in hard times. This is the story within that song.

The tiny Cornish village of Mousehole stands on the Penryn Peninsula, not far from the fishing ports of Newlyn and Penzance. Being as far in the south-west of Cornwall as it's possible to venture without getting your feet wet, it is not surprising that Mousehole gets some of the wildest weather that the Atlantic can throw at it.

Many years ago one Cornish winter saw particularly bad winds; as the fishermen would say, 'It was blowing a hooley.' For the whole of November the gales were so bad that even the weather-hardened fishermen couldn't put to sea. Christmas was fast approaching and the families of the fishermen were getting desperate. No fish meant little to eat and no money. In every fishing community there is an old 'salt' to whom the young bloods look for the decision about whether it's safe to go to sea. There is also often a stubborn old 'salt' who will venture out when nobody else dares to leave the port. At the end of the second week in December, Tom Bawcock stood on the harbour wall and announced, to anybody who cared to listen, that he would go to sea at first light on the morning tide whatever the weather.

The following morning at half-light there was just one swinging lantern being carried down the steep hill from the dotted fishermen's cottages to the harbour. Tom Bawcock was going to sea! Indeed, he was the only one daring to go to sea. He was determined that the good people of Mousehole wouldn't go without that Christmas. Even though the wind had eased slightly, it was still blowing a gale. Tom shot his net. An hour later, when he hauled the net, he was disappointed to discover in the cod end of the trawl a selection of the kind of fish that Cornish fishermen would usually only use as bait in their crab or lobster pots. There were seven different kinds of fish: gurnard, horse mackerel, whiting, a small conger eel, a tiny codling, a small skate and some Cornish 'silver darlings' (pilchards). Not a great catch, but nevertheless a feed of fresh fish. Like most fishermen, Tom knew well how to prepare and cook such a catch. As he looked into the basket of fish thoughtfully, an enormous gust of wind and a giant wave knocked him over backward on the slippery deck. As conditions were worsening, Tom decided not to push his luck, although he thought it was a pity to head back leaving fish down there in the wet!

Tom moored securely at the tiny quayside and set off up the steep hill with the basket of fish on his back, to the cheers of the locals. This was a community who looked after each other and tonight they would all eat. The baker made a huge batch of wholemeal bread. On the way home Tom borrowed the biggest pie dish in the village. As soon as he was home, he lit the oven and then made a large bowl of pastry, rolling it out to line the pie dish. He prepared and cooked six different kinds of fish for the filling, keeping the pilchards and a ball of pastry for the pie's crowning glory.

Making a lid for the pie, he cut slits in the lid, pushing a pilchard into each slit with heads and eyes facing upwards towards the stars (hence the term Stargazey). This was not done for effect, although it did look strange and magical, but rather so that the rich oil, the most nutritious and sustaining part of this small fish, could drizzle down into the pie filling.

All the villagers crammed into Tom's little cottage that night and all ate well for the first time in weeks.

To this day, in December on Tom Bawcock's Eve (7 December), Mousehole people gather in the pub by the harbour to sing and eat Stargazey pie in the lead-up to Christmas.

A finer place you'd never believe
Than Mousehole on Tom Bawcock's Eve.

Smugglers' Rum Butter

Lakeland can be a bleak place in the depths of winter. From November to February folk living in the coastal villages can be chilled to the marrow. At times of extreme cold and cutting winds the farmers and fishermen – or even the local priest or vicar – enjoy the comfort of some strong liquor to warm the cockles of their hearts. The spirit of choice in this remote part of England is rum. This choice probably dates back to the dark history of the slave trade between English ports and the Caribbean, which thankfully was finally put to an end by Wilberforce and others. The cargo of these tall ships also contained rum, sugar and spice, which all became integral to the food to be found in the kitchens of this region.

Many years ago, one dark and misty night, a group of folk from a village on the Cumbrian coast – including the local vicar, who was partial to a tot of rum – waited in a small boat just offshore for the delivery of a barrel of rum, a sack of brown sugar and some precious spices. They drew alongside the enormous ship and the goods were gently lowered into their small boat. These smugglers, for that's what they were, rowed for the shore as the ship turned and headed towards Whitehaven harbour to end its voyage.

No sooner had the smugglers landed their precious goods on the shore when on the far clifftop they spotted the light of lanterns and heard the distant sound of voices. Could it be the customs and excise men? They were in trouble! Quickly, and under the cover of darkness, they carried the goods in to a small cave under the cliff. Deep in the cave, on a large flat stone, they came across a tub of butter. This must have been the place that the nearest farmer's wife used to store her produce to keep it cool – no refrigerators in those days! They placed their gains next to the tub of butter and, sitting around the rum barrel, discussed their next move. They turned to the vicar for advice, who suggested that they should sit it out until the customs men, if that's who they were, gave up and turned back to the town. They may need to stay there for the rest of the night.

Now these were mostly big, strong men used to heavy work, with an appetite to match, and they were hungry. Some of them had not even had supper before leaving home. What could they do to sustain themselves through the night? Needs must, they would have to turn to the ingredients they had to hand. They would need to use some of their ill-gotten gains. Mixing together some of the rum, sugar and spices into the butter in the tub, they had unwittingly made the first ever 'Rum Butter'. Spreading dollops of this on to the few biscuits that one of them had brought with him in his pocket, they shared them and so survived a long night, maybe even sharing a warming tot of rum as well!

Peering out of the cave with the first light of morning, the men were delighted to discover that there was no sign of any customs men or indeed of anyone. So quickly and quietly they gathered their gains and returned to their homes. The story of how they had come to invent rum butter soon spread and folk tried it for themselves. In fact, rum butter even came to hold a special place in their hearts. It even became part of christening celebrations, and to this day is still given to babies at christenings as they say 'butter shows them the richness of life, sugar the sweetness of life, spices represent the spice of life, and the rum ... the spirit of life'. They even have special rum butter pots at the christening that, once emptied, are filled with coins for the baby.

You too might like to make rum butter to celebrate the spirit of life, perhaps spreading it on Grasmere gingerbread, mince pies or even a slice of Christmas pudding.

Davy and the King of the Fishes

I once enjoyed a year working with Padstow fisherman Tommy Morrisey as his crew in the final year of his working life. In return for my help, he gave me fish, songs and stories, a wonderful way to add to my repertoire of tales. Naturally my staple diet consisted of fish, my favourite being mackerel, fresh from the sea. 'The sun should never set on a mackerel!' as Tommy would say, so this story just had to be in this collection.

The only job that Davy could find, at the age of 18, was working for an old fisherman. Every day, when they went to sea and the skipper dumped the catch on the deck, Davy's job was cutting off fish heads and taking out the guts – the squidgy bits in the middle. Davy hated that part of the work.

One fine day at sea, the skipper dumped a mackerel on the deck for gutting. Davy admired its beautiful stripes and bright eyes. When he felt the fish wriggling in his hands he couldn't bring himself to kill it. So he hid it behind his back, and when he thought the skipper wasn't looking, he slipped it back over the side of the boat into the sea. He gave it its life.

But the skipper had seen, and there was a terrible row. The old man pointed out that he didn't go to sea every day, getting soaked to the skin catching fish to scrape a living, for the boy to throw them back.

Davy stood before the mast, whistling. Now you never whistle on a fishing boat, for if you do, you're either whistling up the wind or you're whistling up the devil. This made the skipper even more furious. In fact, he sacked Davy on the spot, telling him that when they returned to the port, he must leave the boat and never set foot on it again.

Davy was half-glad and he was half-sad. He was half-glad because he hated the job anyway, and he was half-sad because he knew he was going to have to go home and tell his wife he was out of work again.

He left the boat, climbing the ladder to the quayside, his eyes filled with tears and the corners of his mouth turned down. On the walk home, Davy realised he'd got company: there was a strange man walking beside him, leading a black and white Friesian cow. If Davy had looked carefully he would have noticed two little horns on the top of the stranger's head and a red tail sticking out of the back of his trousers. Of course, it was Old Nick, Old Scratch … The devil himself!

The devil asked why Davy looked so sad. Davy told the stranger that he had lost his job and that he was going to have to go home and tell his wife … he was in big trouble.

The devil told Davy that if he owned the black and white cow he wouldn't be out of work because the cow gave the richest and creamiest milk there has ever been: Davy and his wife could make butter, cheese and ice cream and open a tea shop, something they'd always fancied doing.

The devil made a bargain with Davy, telling him that he could borrow the cow for three years. However, when he returned to collect it he would ask Davy three questions. If Davy couldn't answer them, he would be thrown over the devil's shoulder and carried away to burn in the fires of hell.

To Davy, three years seemed a long way off. Besides, at the age of 18 he thought himself invincible. He shook hands with the devil and the bargain was struck. The devil handed Davy the rope, which was tied around the cow's neck, and headed for home. As the devil did a double somersault and disappeared through a crack in the earth, Davy thought he would never set eyes on him again.

Davy's wife was looking out through the kitchen window. When she saw her husband walking up the lane, leading a black and white cow, she was amazed. Davy had brought home friends before, he'd bought home fish before; but he'd never before brought home a cow.

She rushed out to meet him and asked what was going on. Proudly, Davy told her that the cow gave the richest and creamiest milk there's ever been, and they were going to open a tea shop, for he had packed in the fishing.

The news of Davy and his wife's tea shop soon spread – like the butter itself – and they did very well.

But three years to the day after the bargain was struck with the devil, Davy was in the tea shop mopping the floor, with just one customer – a stranger – sitting in the corner.

Suddenly, there was a flash of blue light and there appeared Old Nick, Old Scratch … the devil himself. He'd polished his skin up bright red and sharpened his hooves and his tail specially. He looked menacingly at Davy, telling him he'd come to collect the cow but, even worse, he had three questions that Davy had to answer. If he couldn't answer them, he would be over the devil's shoulder and down to the fires of hell.

He asked if Davy was ready to answer the questions. But, before Davy could utter a word, the stranger in the corner answered that Davy was ready and that the devil had just asked his first question.

Getting slightly niggled, the devil asked if the stranger in the corner would butt out. Quickly, the stranger retorted that he wouldn't, and that the devil had now asked his second question.

Irritably, the devil asked who this interfering stranger was. The stranger replied that he was the King of the Fishes. Three years ago Davy had thrown him back over the side of the boat, saving his life, and now he had come to repay Davy for his kindness. Not only this, but the devil had just asked his third and final question.

The devil realised he had been outwitted and, in a tantrum, stamped his hoof on the ground, making a hoof print in the concrete. He stormed out of the tea shop in a sulk. In fact, he was in such a sulk he clean forgot to collect his cow.

As far as I know, Davy and his wife are still there, so if you're ever in a tea shop by the seaside, have a glance around the floor, and if you can spot a hoof print in the concrete, you're in the tea shop that Davy and his wife are running to this very day. The last time I was there, the dish of the day on the blackboard was devilled mackerel! If you get to visit you might even be lucky enough to try a dish of ice cream made from the milk of that black and white Friesian cow.

Petit Fours

These tasty treats are the traditional end to a good meal. The following are four short anecdotes that may also prove to be 'tall'. I doubt if you'll find any of these in any other folklore, folk tale or food history collection as they are from the 'library of my (the Author's) mind'.

They are four short tasters, that could be more expansive but are served here stripped to the bone, in order to give my readers some trivia to share at dinner parties or at their storyteller's suppers. So pass them on.

1. It's an Ill Wind …

> Of all the fish that live in the sea
> The herring's the king of the fish for me.

Benjamin Collingwood was a simple in-shore fisherman who launched his coble daily from the beach at Craster to net herring in the North Sea. One day, coming ashore with a haul of the 'silver darlings', he beached his coble and lugged his wooden pallet of the fish up the beach to his shed. He placed the tray of fish on a shelf above the anchors, buoys and nets he stored there, and then made his way up to the Anchor Bar for a swift pint and a slow smoke of his pipe.

Later, on his way back to his tiny cottage he paused on the beach to check the tide and knock the dottle from his pipe on the side of his old shed. Without noticing the shower of sparks flying, he strode up to his cottage, boots off and straight to sleep. In the middle of the night he was woken by the knocking at his door of a neighbour who had come to tell him that his shed was on fire.

Pulling on his boots, he raced down to the shed to find it burnt beyond repair. The previous day's catch, however, wasn't burnt black; rather the fish had 'hot smoked' in the oak wood shed, turning it a rich amber colour and giving it a strong, pleasant smell. Ben couldn't resist tasting a mouthful of one of the fillets, and it was rather fine. So it was that a new way of preparing herring was born. As this had happened while the fisherman had been having a 'kip', you can work out for yourself what this new dish came to be called …!

2. Fast Food

Run rabbit, run rabbit, run, run, run …

In the midst of the Second World War the Devonshire Regiment was posted to Catterick Barracks in Yorkshire for training. The food in the mess was shocking, so the lads decided to take matters into their own hands. Pinching strings from an unplayable old piano in the mess, they fashioned snares and made their way up on to the moors.

These were Dartmoor 'hunter-gatherers' and after a couple of hours they returned with a catch of half a dozen wild rabbits. They knew well how to prepare the game and, with the help of the mess cook, a large pan of delicious rabbit stew was bubbling away. At dinner, one of the barrack's officers commented that it was wonderful 'tucker' and wished to know what the meat was. One of the Dartmoor lads, Private Ray Tucker, told him that they knew it as 'underground mutton'. The officer enquired how he might acquire some of this 'underground mutton'. The private advised him to go up on to the moor with a large stick, find a hole in the banking, raise the stick and make a noise like a carrot! Then when a pair of long furry ears appeared he should bring the stick down sharply and 'thwack', mission should be accomplished!

3. A Happy Accident

Don't upset the apple cart

Two sisters, Stephanie and Caroline Tatin, together ran a small hotel just south of Paris. They always took turns to cook for each other. Stephanie had the cold hands that made her the best baker. One day she had arranged circles of apples on her pastry and sprinkled it generously with sugar to make an apple tart, which she placed in the hot oven. During the time the tart was cooking she became distracted by thoughts of other jobs she had to do. Consequently, as she lifted the hot tart from the oven, with her mind on other things, she let it fall upside down on to the hot plate on top of the oven.

Distressed, Stephanie didn't just scrape it up to bin it, she reached for a large spatula and gingerly tried turning it over, apple side upwards. She arranged the apple slices back in to shape and noticed that while face down on the hot plate the apple had caramelised, turning it a pleasing golden colour. Nothing ventured … she called her sister to the kitchen and cut two slices of the sweet-smelling tart, dressing each slice with Chantilly cream; and didn't the two sisters agree it tasted 'tres bon'.

Of course, Stephanie never told of her 'faux pas', and 'tarte tatin' became a famous classic of French cuisine.

4. Betsy's Bar

A cocktail party

The eighteenth century saw the days of the American War of Independence. The English redcoats in Virginia, whenever possible, would slip out of the barracks for a crafty drink at the bar of one Betsy Flanagan. Betsy regularly served them a potent concoction of strong spirits and mixers. As soon as the soldiers were settled, she dispatched her husband and sons round to the barracks to steal poultry from the chicken shed by the kitchen. When they returned with their ill-gotten gains, the spoils would be plucked and prepared to make southern fried chicken, her speciality dish, which she sold at the bar. The feathers of the cockerels, however, were used to decorate the glasses of the fancy drinks she served to the soldiers.

With their feather decorations, the popular drinks came to be known as cocktails and they even probably hampered the Redcoats' ability to do well in battle the following morning. Cocktails still remain popular to this day and continue to debilitate those who overindulge.

EPILOGUE

After a supper spiced with stories, we should celebrate with a well-spiced drink. My choice would be the juice of the apple thanks to a fond memory from fifty years ago when I encountered the legendary Somerset storyteller Ruth Tongue, who told me this story, our last tale at this Storyteller's Supper.

The Apple Tree Man

When Somerset storyteller and folklorist Ruth Tongue was a child she wandered into an orchard with a friend. Gazing at an ancient gnarled apple tree, the young companion told Ruth it was the 'Apple Tree Man'. This fed Ruth's imagination and when I was taken to meet her in the 1970s she told me the stories of 'Tibb's Cat' and the 'The Apple Tree Man', two stories that tell of this venerable tree sprite. Over the years of my storytelling, these two tales have melded into one. The dialect is kept in the following version as it is the poetry of the country people that I grew up with on my maternal grandfather's farm, where lunches in the field often consisted of bread, cheese, a raw onion and a cup of cider ... even for us boys!

There was this hard-working chap, as was the eldest of a long family, so when his dad died there weren't nothing left for ee, the youngest brother gets it all as ee would be fitter to work the farm, if he hadn't been such a lazy spoilt young hosebird. All he do let the oldest brother have was his dad's old dunk (that's a donkey), an ox that had gone to a natomy (that's a skeleton) and a tumble-down cottage with two or dree ancient old apple trees where his dad had used to live to with his grandfer. The oldest brother ee didn't grumble as a lot of folks would, no he went cutting the grass along the lane, and he fed it to the dunk, and the old dunk began to fatten up and walk smart. Then he rubbed the ox's side with herbs and said the words, magic words, and the old ox began to perk himself up. They old apple trees began to flourish a marvel with the beasts being in the orchard. All this work didn't leave the older brother time to find his rent: O yes, youngest brother had to have his rent, dap on the dot too, greedy young guzzle bag!

One day the youngest brother stormed into the orchard and muttered 'tomorrow 'twill be Christmas Eve when beasts do talk, we all know there's a treasure buried hereabouts and I am all set to ask your dunk and your ox where 'tis hid to. Wake me up just afore midnight and I'll knock a whole sixpence off your rent,' and off he goes, greedy young hosebird.

Well, as I said the following day was Christmas Eve and come nightfall who should come wandering into the orchard but the little cat from down Tibb's farm. Not much more than a kitten she were, a dairy maid of a cat (that's a black cat that's dipped her nose in a saucer of cream), and you know what they say about curiosity and the cat! So ere er was in the orchard, owl-light on Christmas Eve, when out popped the Apple Tree Man! The Apple Tree Man shouted, 'You git on home my dear, this be no place for you, there's folk coming tonight to fire guns drew my branches and pour cider drew my roots, wassailers … you git on home and don't ee come back yer again until St Tibb's Eve.'

The little kitten shot off with her tail stiff with fright,

properly scared she the Apple Tree Man did, and er never went back in the orchard again cos er didn't know when St Tibb's Eve were! You and I know 'tis the night before St Tibb's Day!

Whilst all this were gain on, the older brother he put a sprig of holly up in the Shippen (that's the cow shed) and gave his dunk and his ox a bit extra food to last them through Christmas day 'cos he weren't gain to work that day. Then he took his last jug of cider and mulled it in front of the ashen faggot, then out to the orchard to give it to the apple tree. His was just pouring the cider down drew the roots when out popped the Apple Tree Man. The Apple Tree Man shouted, 'You look under this gurt didocky root of mine and you'll find something to do ee a bit of good.' So he looked under the root and he found a chest of the finest gold. 'Tis yourn and no-one else's,' said the Apple Tree Man; 'you put it away safe and bide quiet about en. Now you can call your dear brother and tell him 'tis midnight.'

Well the youngest brother came rushing out into the orchard in a terrible hurry push, and sure enough the dunk was talking to the ox, 'You do mind thic gurt greedy fool that's listening to we so unmannerly – ee do want we should tell ee where the treasure's hid to.'

'And that's where ee ain't gonna get it,' said the ox, 'as somebody 'ave took ee already.' And do you know that was the last words they two beasts ever spoke. However, even to this day in the West Country we still:

> Wassail the trees that they may bear
> Many an apple and many a pear,
> For the more or less fruit they will bring,
> As we do give them wassailing.

Taffy's Wassail Recipe

Ingredients

1 pint dry cider (or apple juice)
Slice of root ginger
½ cinnamon stick
2 tbsp soft brown sugar
6 cloves
Fresh grated nutmeg

Method

1. Combine ingredients in a saucepan over a medium heat.
2. Stir with a wooden spoon.
3. If serving in a punch bowl, float roasted apple on top.

'Cinnamon, ginger, nutmeg and cloves and cider gave me my jolly red nose.' Wassail or 'Wes Hale' in old English means 'Be whole or Good health', as in 'hale and hearty'. Carollers singing wassail songs are wishing folk well over Christmas and New Year. However, in areas famous for their apple orchards, the custom is to wassail the apple trees. Healthy apple trees mean more apples and more apples mean more apple juice and that means more … cider!

Wassailers visit apple trees with this mixture in a wassail cup, decorating the branches with buttered toast to feed the robins, who bring good luck. They also create a loud noise to frighten away any evil spirits while pouring a little from the cup into the roots and then sharing the rest. Perhaps these old customs where folk gather to celebrate with food and drink build a sense of well-being that enables them to create their own luck.

A FAREWELL TOAST

Take the road
Warm with words
From many a merry tale
Raise a glass to one and all
Just one last toast
Wassail!

TT

BIBLIOGRAPHY

As you will discover, many of the sources of my tales are oral and often credited in the introductions to them. However, I sometimes delve into my trusty archive of favourite books for ideas and inspiration.

Barber, A., and Hess, P., *Hidden Tales from Eastern Europe*, 2002.

Briggs, Katharine M., *A Dictionary of British Folk Tales*, 1970.

Grimm, J. and W., (trans. by Mrs Edgar Lucas, illust. by Arthur Rackham) *Fairy Tales of the Brothers Grimm*, 1909.

Holt, D., and Mooney, B., *More Ready to Tell Tales*, 2000.

Jacobs, J., *English Fairy Tales*, 1890.

Keding, D., *Elder Tales*, 2008.

Potter, B., *The Fairy Caravan*, 1929.

Tongue, R., *Forgotten Folk Tales of the English Counties*, 1970.

Society *for*
Storytelling

Since 1993, The Society for Storytelling has championed the ancient art of oral storytelling and its long and honourable history – not just as entertainment, but also in education, health, and inspiring and changing lives. Storytellers, enthusiasts and academics support and are supported by this registered charity to ensure the art is nurtured and developed throughout the UK.

Many activities of the Society are available to all, such as locating storytellers on the Society website, taking part in our annual National Storytelling Week at the start of every February, purchasing our quarterly magazine Storylines, or attending our Annual Gathering – a chance to revel in engaging performances, inspiring workshops, and the company of like-minded people.

You can also become a member of the Society to support the work we do. In return, you receive free access to Storylines, discounted tickets to the Annual Gathering and other storytelling events, the opportunity to join our mentorship scheme for new storytellers, and more. Among our great deals for members is a 30% discount off titles from The History Press.

For more information, including how to join, please visit

www.sfs.org.uk

The destination for history
www.thehistorypress.co.uk